W9-AUP-297

ORGANIZE YOUR HOME OFFICE!

SIMPLE ROUTINES
FOR SETTING UP AN
OFFICE AT HOME

ORGANIZE YOUR HOME OFFICE!

SIMPLE ROUTINES FOR SETTING UP AN OFFICE AT HOME

RONNI EISENBERG WITH KATE KELLY

HYPERION

NEW YORK

Library of Congress Cataloging-in-Publication Data

Eisenberg, Ronni.
    Organize your home office : simple routines for setting up an office at
home / Ronni Eisenberg with Kate Kelly.—1st ed.
        p.   cm.
    1. Office layout.   2. Home offices.   I. Kelly, Kate
    HF5547.2.E37   2000
    658.2'3—dc21   99-34677
                                                        CIP

ISBN 0-7868-8465-7
First Edition
10   9   8   7   6   5   4   3   2

Design by Robert Bull Design

CONTENTS

ORGANIZE YOUR HOME OFFICE!

SIMPLE ROUTINES FOR SETTING UP AN OFFICE AT HOME

Introduction

Today more than one third of all working Americans (that's roughly 40 million people) have an office at home. Some are running a home-based business or telecommuting while others are freelancing or just trying to find a quiet place to pay the bills. But setting up a home office and keeping it running smoothly can be a job in itself.

In *Organize Your Home Office!* you'll find suggestions about every aspect of setting up shop in a spare room, garage, or a handy corner. There is also invaluable advice on everything from purchasing the right equipment and using the Internet to coping with distractions and interruptions.

Whether you're a professional, a telecommuter, a student, an entrepreneur, or someone who simply needs a place to do desk work at home, this book will help ensure that you'll run your operation as smoothly as any corporate executive.

Here's what you have to have to make it work:

1. **You have to be motivated.** Working from home takes discipline, and you have to *want* to work there. Isolation and family distractions make it virtually impossible for some personalities to work at home. You can create a decorator-style home office, but if you're not prepared to arm yourself with self-discipline and the will to fight off distractions, it will never work.

2. **You need to dedicate space for a home office.** That space can be as

compact as a file drawer and table that you use as a desk or it can be a full room outfitted with lots of business equipment. Don't even *think* of working at your kitchen table! You'll be in the midst of accomplishing some work and then you'll have to pick up everything because the table is needed for a meal.

3. **You need to master the art of time management and become skilled at staying organized.** Home offices are wonderful places but most lack "pick-up squads" and secretaries. This means that it is up to you, and you alone, to set up systems (with help from this book, of course) so that you'll get to your appointments on time, follow up with clients as needed, and be able to put your hands on the necessary papers at the right time.

HOW TO USE THIS BOOK

A quick scan of the table of contents shows you that this book begins at the beginning with how to set up a home office and proceeds with everything you need to work successfully from home.

For those of you who have never had a home office, start from the beginning and read right through, turning down corners, underlining, and highlighting anything you want to remember. That way you can refer back to various sections when you need them, rereading the filing chapter when you're ready to set up your new files, or setting up a "mobile office" when you're on the road a great deal.

Those of you who already work from home can read more selectively. Use the table of contents to go directly to the subjects that are of the most interest to you. There will be suggestions that help you manage your time, balance work and family, and keep your life organized.

In my opinion, there's no greater place to work than at home. Enjoy.

PART ONE

PRACTICAL MATTERS

1
WORKING FROM HOME:
IS IT FOR YOU?

WHAT'S AHEAD

Is Working from Home for You? A Quiz
The Benefits
The Drawbacks

For many people, working from home sounds like paradise—you get up when you want, put on some coffee, wander to your desk after reading the paper and walking the dog, and then you settle down and get some work done before taking a break for lunch.

There are many benefits to working from home, but any person who has tried it will tell you that it takes great self-discipline and determination to get anything done. For that reason, working from home isn't for everybody. There's something to be said for the workplace-imposed discipline of getting up in the morning and working at an office where co-workers might notice if you drifted in at 11:00 A.M. in your pajamas. Even entrepreneurs sometimes opt for office space outside the house simply because they aren't prepared to wrestle to keep the kids off the office computer, the dog quiet during phone calls, and to avoid having to run all the family errands because "you've got lots of free time during the day."

However, for an increasing number of people, working from home offers many advantages. The entrepreneur saves on overhead and enjoys many conveniences; the telecommuter finds that he or she can participate in family activities to a greater extent than working on site for a company for forty hours per week; and the moonlighter finds that extra moments are available for earning extra income.

Try taking this short quiz to see if you're temperamentally suited for working at home.

IS WORKING FROM HOME FOR YOU? A QUIZ

True/False

1. You are well organized.

2. You work well on your own and find that being with others is often distracting.

3. You enjoy the company of others but don't find that seeing people is necessary to make each day complete.

4. You have considered what it will mean to your family if you cannot be disturbed during certain hours of the day.

5. Your home or apartment can be set up in such a way that you can work undisturbed and/or have business materials that will remain undisturbed.

6. You have enough self-confidence in what you're doing that you'll be able to take your work seriously even when things are slow.

7. You're good at creating and working through "to do" lists even when there are other things tugging at your time.

8. You enjoy your work but know when it's time to stop.

9. You feel relatively certain that you can tame the call of the refrigerator, the lure of walking the dog, and even odd urgent desires to "tidy up" before settling down to work.

10. You are aware of the need for a support system and have some ideas of what you could set up for yourself.

If you answered true to most of the above questions, then you are an excellent candidate for working from home, whether as a telecommuter or as an entrepreneur. But before you make any hasty moves, take a look at both the benefits and drawbacks of setting up an office at home.

THE BENEFITS

Freedom, flexibility, time-savings, and control are certainly key benefits to working from home. Consider the specifics:

You're in charge. This has as much to do with being your own boss as it does with working from home, but the bottom line is that *you* dictate what type of work you do, how you run things, and how much or how little time you devote to everything—a nice way to feel good about what you're doing.

You can set your hours according to your needs. If you're a night person or if you need to accomplish all your work during the school day, you are now able to establish a work schedule that works best for you.

You can set your own "vacation" time and compensate before or after. At times when you're frantically busy, you'll likely be working around the clock, just as you would be if you worked in a corporation, but if you're not so busy, and the weather's beautiful, you can knock off for the afternoon and take advantage of it.

You can keep costs down. Many entrepreneurs start out working from home for the very simple reason that it saves money.

You'll save on commuting time. Whether you drove or took public transportation to a previous job, working from home gives you back that time. You may still have to travel to meet clients or attend meetings, but chances are your time investment will be less. Since you may be able to travel at off-hours and you're not commuting regularly, you'll save a good deal of time each week.

Work is less likely to keep you away from family events. While working from home doesn't mean you'll be at every soccer game, it does mean that you have more flexibility to participate in your children's schedules and try to be there for the things that are important to all of you.

You become a part of your home community. People who have previously commuted into major cities find that joining a local networking group or serving on a town committee is a way to spend time with business associates who are neighbors. They find this preferable to the impersonal contacts made in large cities.

THE DRAWBACKS

For many people, the benefits outweigh the drawbacks, but before embarking on a new life working at home, it's important to understand that there are some disadvantages as well:

Working from home requires enormous self-discipline. If you're a major procrastinator or work best when "the boss" is hovering nearby, then you may need to think twice about creating a home-based career. Time management and self-mastery are vital ingredients to succeeding—and to feeling good about working from home. If you're constantly annoyed at yourself for something you didn't do but meant to do, frustration will mar any enjoyment that working from home might offer.

You need to invest in setting up an office. For most people, working from home isn't something to do that will "tide you through a couple of months." A good home office requires an investment in equipment, and proper space must be devoted to provide a decent work environment. The days of launching businesses from a kitchen table are long gone—clients (or your corporate boss if you're telecommuting) expect home-based workers to produce documents on computer, be able to respond to e-mail, and have fax machines as well. In other words, setting up a home office is a big deal. And if you expect to see clients at home, it's even more important that you establish an environment that frees you from worrying about "how the house looks." Some home-based businesses set up their homes so that there is a separate entrance and a special waiting area, in addition to a separate office, so this adds to the cost.

You're isolated. Probably the single biggest adjustment people have to make when they start working from home is getting used to being alone. This hurdle is entirely surmountable—you can establish a schedule that builds in professional "people" time regularly, and the Internet has greatly reduced people's feelings of isolation. The loneliness issue, however, still must be addressed. (Some people are perfectly happy with the fact that they can work single-mindedly to accomplish their tasks and then quit work to meet someone for a tennis game, but others really miss the camaraderie of the office water cooler.)

There can be a lack of security/privacy. Whether or not security and privacy are issues for you depends on the nature of your business. For most, it won't be a deciding factor as to whether or not you work from home since alternative arrangements can often be made. For example, if you're a copywriter, you can visit clients in their offices, a service they may expect anyway. Or you can arrange off-site meetings in restaurants or hotel lobbies. If, however, your profession is client-intensive and you must see people regularly, it will be more cost-effective to be able to see them in your own home office. You'll need to accept the fact that people will be coming and going from your home.

People don't take you seriously. Clients are sometimes skeptical of someone who isn't in an office setting. You can generally overcome this hurdle by proving yourself on a professional basis and then making certain that your toddler doesn't pick up your business line and that the sound of barking dogs is out of range of your office.

You'll also find that friends and family members have trouble understanding the concept of "working" at home. Perhaps because other people have difficulty being purposeful at home, they fail to understand that you might be doing something serious. Questions like, "Do you want to go for coffee, take a walk, go for a jog, attend a store sale with me?" are common. You'll also hear: "You're at home. Why *can't* you help out with the school play?" Then there will be the mid-morning call from a neighborhood friend saying, "What's new?" All this gives a strong indication that people assume you work at home "when there's nothing else to do."

Lack of structure and support. People who prefer a structured environment are less likely to be happy working at home, simply because it's harder to create one's own structure. Places with structure (company offices) also offer support in the way of phone coverage, clerical help, and other types of office services. When you work from home, you'll find that you'll either need to do these things for yourself or hire a person or a service to do it for you.

Different child-care needs. If you have children, working from home may actually complicate your child-care situation. If they are with an at-home caregiver, you need the space to accommodate your office as well as the children's play in another part of the house. Caregivers often complain that it's more difficult for them to establish themselves as the authority figure when a parent is nearby, so you need to be careful not to undermine that. (The last thing you want to do while working is become the arbitrator in some household dispute.) If your children are in school or they are already attending a daycare center, you may find that having them out of the house during your work hours offers the best alternative for all of you.

You may have difficulty separating work and home. An advantage of striding off to work each day is that it's very clear which is work and which is home. When you venture to an upstairs office with a cup of coffee from your own kitchen, the line is less clear. This difficulty affects people both ways: Some have difficulty settling down to work because they find the call of the refrigerator or the need to rearrange the linen closet more powerful than the desire to work. Others find it impossible to close the office door nights and weekends, and they find that they no longer have leisure time—whenever they have a spare second they're back in their office trying to get something done.

None of these drawbacks are insurmountable, but before you start investing in the time and expense of setting up a home office, you need to be aware of both the pluses and the minuses.

In all likelihood, however, you were vaguely aware of some of the challenges before you bought this book and are prepared to make the commitment. If so, your first steps involve making sure you're operating legally and identifying the correct space.

2

THE BUSINESS SIDE OF ESTABLISHING A HOME OFFICE

WHAT'S AHEAD

Operating Legally
Rules, Permits, and Regulations
Financial Issues
Insurance

This chapter might better be titled, "Home Office Owner Beware!" Even the nicest neighbors may get up in arms once they hear that you're going to use your newly acquired license in social work to begin to see patients at home. Or if your business involves a product, you may find that Nosy Neighbor on Your Right suddenly decides you'll be receiving deliveries through the night, and Nosy Neighbor on Your Left wants to be certain that no one will ever park anywhere near his property.

Suffice it to say that unless your home office is going to be used purely for bill-paying, it's vital that you take care of the legalities of setting up your home office so that you can keep on doing business through the years. Even a moonlighter or telecommuter needs to find out what is necessary to legalize a home office in his or her community. Home-based artists and writers who barely stick their noses outside may think they have nothing to fear, but if a neighbor has her nose out of joint about something you said or did, your home office can be closed down as quickly as the one who is selling antiques out of a basement showroom.

OPERATING LEGALLY

- Because every community has different laws, your first call should be to your county or city clerk to ask what requirements, if any, might apply to your home office. In all likelihood, there will be little that you need to do.

- If a community has any sort of interest in a home office/business at all, it will primarily be concerned with the following issues:

  —Amount of traffic generated. An occasional car (or even a delivery truck now and then) shouldn't be a problem, but if your home office is being created to operate a business that relies on people coming to you regularly, you may want to think twice about operating from home. If you do foresee regular traffic, consider what parking you can provide. The client/patient/associate whose car can be pulled directly into your driveway shouldn't be a problem in most neighborhoods.

  —Number of employees. Again, parking and congestion are the major issues here.

  —Outside signage is generally prohibited or will in most cases be subject to approval of a local board.

  —The use of a home office and the presence of a home business should not bring with it bad smells, an unusual amount of noise, or unsightly waste.

  —To maintain a residential feel, it's important that homes remain residences. Governing boards want to be reassured that the house is your home first and its *secondary* use is as a place of business.

RULES, PERMITS, AND REGULATIONS

- Some communities may require business permits or licenses. Again, the city or county clerk will be able to tell you what you need to know.

- Police permits are sometimes required if there will be an increase in traffic; the sanitation and fire departments may also have specifications you have to meet.

- Some communities may have zoning laws with which you must comply. These restrictions are to protect the rights of the neighbors and to assure the safety of their property. No one—including you—would want to live next door to a home where big trucks arrived at 7 A.M. to pick up merchandise for delivery, or where cooking smells wafted through the neighborhood because a home office ran a home-based catering service as well.

- Other regulations depend on the nature of your business. For example, if you prepare food, you must comply with county health department codes.

- If you live in an apartment building or co-op or within a neighborhood that has an active neighborhood association, you'll want to check to see if there are any rules or regulations with which you must comply.

FINANCIAL ISSUES

- Establish a business bank account.

- Plan ahead for the tax man. Create your tax categories at the beginning of the year and record your expenses regularly. Use an accordion file to hold all tax-related documents and receipts.

- Back up your computer system regularly and keep paper printouts of your financial information. If your computer should crash you'll still have the documents you need for the IRS.

INSURANCE

- Investigate what to do about insurance. Though you may be able to get the coverage you need through your homeowner's policy, there is very little automatic coverage, so discuss with your insurance agent what coverage you will need for a home office. There are two specific types of insurance to keep in mind.

  —**Property insurance.** This type of insurance covers losses arising from physical damage, loss of use of the property (such as from fire), and theft. Talk to your insurance agent about insuring the contents of your home office. A lot of money can be tied up in machinery and equipment, inventory, and business records. You may be able to cover this under your homeowner's policy, but if not, take out additional insurance to be certain you're covered.

— **Liability insurance.** This type of insurance protects you if you are sued for accidents in your place of business. If an employee or customer trips over an area rug, you need to be covered. Some business owners (doctors, lawyers, some types of consultants) also need to carry professional liability insurance to protect against lawsuits that result from professional error, or you might even need coverage in case of lawsuits arising from use of your product. Be sure you have business liability as well as personal liability protection— that's what will provide the protection you need if you're using your home as an office.

• If you're a telecommuter, talk to your employer about insurance coverage. Would the company policy cover any loss or damage to company-supplied equipment? If not, talk to your insurance agent about getting it covered under your policy. A telecommuter should be certain to have liability coverage for a home office under his or her own homeowner's policy, and he or she should still be covered by a company-paid-for workers' compensation policy.

• Save receipts on office equipment and take photographs or a video tape of your home office now and then in order to document what you have. Keep a duplicate of this documentation at another location—a safe deposit box or the home of a relative. The pictures will come in handy if you ever need to file a claim.

- If you'll be using your car for work, tell your insurance agent and obtain an endorsement or a separate policy (depending on the state in which you live). If you've formerly been employed in an office and have been commuting, your agent should be told this as well—you may benefit from a drop in rates if you're no longer commuting regularly.

KEEP IT SIMPLE

1. It's vital that you investigate the legalities of operating a home business in your neighborhood. If you try to skirt the law, the neighbors may trip you up.

2. When it comes to deliveries or parking by clients or employees, be considerate of the neighbors.

3. Call your insurance agent and describe what you're doing. Be sure that you have the proper coverage in the amount you need.

PART TWO

PHYSICAL SPACE AND EQUIPMENT

3
IDENTIFYING YOUR SPACE NEEDS

WHAT'S AHEAD

Deciding What's Important
An Additional (IRS) Consideration
Giving the Area a Test Run
Extra Effort for Extra Space?
If the "Client Issue" Is a Major Problem

You may be surprised to learn that square footage isn't your first consideration when setting up a home office. What's important is whether or not the space you choose is conducive for the kind of work you plan to do. This means factoring in issues such as natural light, sound, and location in relation to the rest of the house. So don't start moving everything out of the spare bedroom you think is just right for your office. It may well be perfect for what you want, but before you start setting up shop in that location, there are important issues to consider.

DECIDING WHAT'S IMPORTANT

1. **What equipment and furniture is essential for the work you do?** Taking this into account is the first step in deciding what your space needs are. In addition to basic office equipment, a graphic artist needs a drawing board, a writer or management consultant will want a computer; a chiropractor or psychiatrist will require space for seeing patients; and a craftsperson may want a worktable.

2. **In what type of environment are you more productive?** Do you need quiet in order to concentrate or are you more comfortable when you have a sense of connectedness? The attic or basement space might be perfect for someone who likes to be apart from the household, but it might feel like exile to someone who prefers to know what's going on throughout the day.

3. **Will clients or patients come to you?** This question is a very important one. The extra bedroom that looked so inviting at first may seem like a poor idea when you consider having patients troop through the family area of the house to get to your office. Instead, you may decide that turning the ground floor den into your office and letting the extra bedroom become a den will make it easier for you to separate family and work—a vital component of working from home. If you have people coming to you regularly, work out a separate entrance and perhaps even a separate waiting room.

4. **Do you and/or your clients require total privacy and/or confidentiality?** While an out-of-the-way location in the household is one way to solve this problem, it can also be resolved in other ways. Soundproofing can be added to surround a room where conversations should not be heard, or an inexpensive sound machine can mask sounds as well.

5. **Do you need to plan for space for an employee? If so, should the employee's desk be near you or in a separate area?** If someone works with you full- or part-time, this will affect the space needed for a home office.

6. **How much time will you spend in your home office, and will it be during the night or during the day?** The moonlighter writing a book in the evening will care less about sunlight than the person who is working full-time from home. And the person who is primarily using the home office to pay bills may think it's convenient to have a

desk near the kitchen where he or she can keep track of what's going on. In contrast, the person who is running a full-time business from home generally needs to be away from family hubbub in order to get work done.

7. **How will other family members' schedules affect your use of the office?** Before selecting a central location for a full-time home office, consider when other family members are around. If you have toddlers who will be with a baby-sitter while you're trying to work, you'll be wise to locate your home office in a more distant part of the house.

8. **If you're considering using a guest bedroom for your office, consider for a moment how frequently you may still need the space for guests.** Being displaced by a visitor can be more disruptive than you might imagine. If you're running a full-time business, it will be aggravating not to be able to function well when you have a visitor. Even if you're not using the office full-time, there's always the privacy issue. How many things might you need to put away if your mother-in-law comes to spend a week with you?

9. **Some professions involve the use of hazardous materials (chemicals for certain types of painting, photography, and printmaking) and may require special clean-up facilities, a particular type of storage to guard against children getting into them, and excellent ventilation.** If you work with materials of this type, choose your location in the household accordingly (an airy room with a sink nearby for easy clean up, or space for safe, high storage).

10. **Do you have a product that must be stored and/or sent out?** If so, you'll need room for storage, and you'll have to create space for packing and materials as well. Keep in mind that for most businesses product storage and mailing needn't be done in the office. You might select a room in the basement for this purpose. In many cases, packages can be prepacked so that you needn't be in the "packing" room daily.

AN ADDITIONAL (IRS) CONSIDERATION

- To qualify for a deduction, the IRS insists that a home office be a separate part of the home and that it be used exclusively as a home office. According to the IRS, you cannot take a home office deduction if your daytime office is also the den where your family watches television at night.

GIVING THE AREA A TEST RUN

- Once you've considered your basic needs, walk around your home and assess where it makes most sense to locate your home office. Move a temporary desk to the area and try working there for a week or two.

- Consider temperature and indoor "climate." This is particularly important if you're considering a formerly unused basement, garage, or attic space where heating or air-conditioning may need to be added in order to make it habitable year-round.

- Consider lighting issues and sound levels. While both of these can also be remedied (lighting can be added to a dark room or curtains can block out glare, and "white noise" can be used to mask annoying sounds). These two issues affect your environment and you may not like what needs to be done to solve them. For example, artificial light is no replacement for sunshine, so if you really like a sunny room then an office in the basement or on the north side of the house isn't for you. And while noise can be masked, it isn't the same as working in a quiet environment.

You'll save yourself time and money if you try out the space first. If you basically like it, it's worth investing in fixing it up.

EXTRA EFFORT FOR EXTRA SPACE?

- If you're still hard-pressed for locating space, consider:
  —Would any of your rooms lend themselves to building a temporary or permanent divider? Dining rooms are often the least-used space in the house, and unless family members

will be traipsing through all day, the area may be perfect for sectioning off for a home office.

—Look around at some of your large closets and small nooks and crannies. Most homes have one or two closets that are big enough to open up to contain a workstation. Check areas under the stairs, and in older homes, take a good look at the butler's pantry.

• Certain problems in other parts of the house can be overcome without too much investment. A dehumidifier in a basement can make a difference in the air quality, and an intercom to either the attic or basement can keep you from feeling isolated. Other projects (skylight for an attic office; finishing off an unfinished basement) are more complex and more costly but permit you to regain space.

• If you're thinking of converting a garage or part of a garage into a home office, consider how you'll feel about being separate from the house. What if you don't hear the doorbell? (An intercom system will remedy this, but at a cost.) Are the children at an age where running out to the office for five minutes will mean that you have to worry about them being alone? And when the weather turns bitter cold, has your garage been weatherproofed well enough that you can continue to use it? (One definite advantage to a garage home office is that you'll feel removed from the home and there are generally fewer distractions in such an environment.)

- After evaluating what's involved and factoring in how much time you'll spend there, you'll be better prepared to evaluate whether or not a major investment is justified. If you decide to undertake construction, talk to at least three contractors or carpenters and get estimates.

IF THE "CLIENT ISSUE" IS A MAJOR PROBLEM

For many families, finding an acceptable location for a home office is relatively easy, unless accommodations must be made for regular visitors. Both security and privacy become concerns at this stage. However, unless your business involves seeing patients or clients on a regular basis, there are very acceptable alternatives to having people come to your home:

—Offer pick-up and delivery services so that clients need never come to you.

—Offer to meet at their place of business.

—Rent an office suite or a conference room for times when you need the space.

—Consider using local hotels and restaurants for your meetings.

KEEP IT SIMPLE

1. Consider your work style, your equipment needs, and your environmental preferences when selecting the optimum location for your home office.

2. Give the space a test run before making any major household changes.

3. If space for meeting with clients is a problem, remember that it's easy enough—often ideal—to meet clients at their own offices or in a hotel lobby. (This type of arrangement has the added benefit of leaving you in control of when the meeting ends.)

	Ample space?	Private?	Quiet?	Convenient?	Not too many distractions?	Okay for visitors?	IRS deduction?
Attic							
Basement							
Butler's pantry							
Den							
Dining area							
Garage							
Guest room							
Kitchen							
Nook/ closet							

4
FURNITURE
FOR THE
HOME OFFICE

WHAT'S AHEAD

Furniture: What to Consider
What You Need Where: A Checklist

Once you've selected the space you plan to use for your home office, then the next step is deciding what furniture you'll need in the room.

In my work, I see all types of home offices, and when it comes to planning out furniture, I think of four offices that were particularly notable:

Office #1 belonged to a talent agent. He had a *huge* desk with so much stuff piled on it (projects, scripts, contracts, letters) that it was hard to tell there was a piece of furniture underneath it all. There was certainly no work space in *this* office.

A photographer—Office #2—was the owner of the *longest* desk I'd seen—ever. She, too, had things piled all over it. It was probably purchased to be a long worktable, but with the way she was using it, "work" was an inoperative word. She also had so many papers and so much photography equipment that it was piled on every chair, so meetings with her were always "stand up." (This is a perfect example of how clutter can expand to fill the space.)

Then there's Office #3 which belonged to a businessman. He told me, "I'm too cheap and too practical to spend money on a desk. This card table is just fine." Seating? A metal folding chair, of course. And the wastebasket? A grocery store bag—with handles. "When it gets full, I just take it out to the trash," he announced proudly. He'd called for advice on getting organized, but I left his office wondering what he did if he needed to see a client in his home office. The next time we spoke, I inquired. His answer: "What any practical businessman would do—I meet them at another location."

Office #4 had a beautiful cherry desk and the entire office was well appointed. So what was the problem? The office belonged to an advertising executive/inventor who kept all his inventions on the desktop and he tinkered with them constantly. For our two-hour meeting, he kept moving around, playing with one item or another. By the end of our meeting, I felt distracted and exhausted.

While how you use the furniture in your office will be discussed elsewhere in the book, having practical, useful furniture is the first step in creating a well-organized office.

FURNITURE: WHAT TO CONSIDER

- **The Desk.** Your desk is the "home base" of any office. Selecting the right one for your needs is important because it determines other furniture selection for the rest of the office.

    The type of desk you choose will be determined by how you plan to use it. In some professions, a large worktable is more practical than a desk because an open work area is needed, so your first decision is whether you want a desk or a table as your work surface. The ideal size desk is generally 66–72 inches with a depth of 36 inches.

    Some people prefer to have their computer on their desk; others want their desk to be a work surface only, with their computer on a separate table nearby. If you opt for putting your computer on your desk, shop for a desk that is deep enough that the computer can sit in a rear corner. (Many desks feature keyboard shelves that slide out of the way when not in use, or you can simply slip the keyboard to the side when you're not using it.) That will permit your desk to perform double duty as a computer table and work surface as well. The desk height should ideally be about 30 inches. The best height for using a keyboard is 26–27 inches, and some desks are made at a standard height of 28 inches in order to be appropriate for all uses.

Consider other features you want in a desk. Before opting for a space-saver style, be certain that you'll still have enough room for your work. Check, too, on drawers. You'll definitely want a pencil drawer to keep pens handy, but many desks feature a three-drawer arrangement with a file-size drawer on the bottom, a drawer that can hold letterhead in the middle, and a pencil drawer at the top.

While an elegant oak rolltop desk or some other type of antique desk offers a great touch to a home office, many people find that antiques aren't as practical as desks that are meant specifically for today's work world. If you find an older piece that serves your needs, terrific, but because space is usually at a premium in home offices you may opt for "efficient" rather than "elegant."

- **Office Chair.** Rather than use an old kitchen chair at your desk, invest in yourself by buying a chair of good quality. If you're going to be in your home office even as little as two hours a day, you'll get your payback in added comfort and reduced fatigue.

Many companies are making ergonomic chairs that are bound to make sitting at a desk, a computer, or a work-table much easier. Look for one with good lower back support, and the height should be set so that your thighs are parallel to the floor when your feet are flat on the ground. If you spend a lot of time at the computer, adjustable armrests can help prevent carpal tunnel syndrome, and a knee-tilt feature lets you tilt forward but still have adequate support for working at the computer. Chair fabric should be something that "breathes" in order to let body heat dissipate. A chair that swivels and that is mounted on sturdy casters lets you move comfortably around a limited area in order to get what you need.

- **Computer and Table.** Unless your computer will sit on your desk, you'll want a computer stand or table. Look for one that is big enough to hold a printer and scanner. Make sure the keyboard will be no higher than 26–28 inches.

- **Work Table or Conference Table.** Your work needs will dictate whether or not you need to plan space for this. Be sure to allow an additional 3–4 feet of space for seating around all sides of the table. This amount of space permits ample room for passage behind those sitting at the table.

- **Equipment.** In addition to a PC, most people today want a fax machine, telephone system, and an answering machine; many also want a home copier. Consider what types of equipment you plan to have so that you can allow enough space for them. (The equipment itself will be explained in detail in Chapter 6.)

Not all your equipment needs to be located in your office; however, this is still the time to plan for what you need and to provide the correct electrical wiring for any equipment you're adding.

- **File Cabinets.** The number of file cabinets you need will depend on how much material you have that must be stored. While you should definitely have a two-drawer unit (at the very least) within your office, more extensive filing cabinets with less frequently needed items can be located in another part of the house to maximize efficient use of a home office. The benefits of different types of file cabinets will be discussed in Chapter 14, but for the purposes of this chapter, you need to consider whether you plan to use a lateral file cabinet or a vertical file cabinet and whether you foresee that it can be tucked into a closet or whether you need to plan for it in your office layout.

  Vertical files are usually 30 inches deep and 15 inches wide for letter-size documents or 18 inches wide for legal-size documents. Vertical files work best when there is limited wall space and adequate space in front of the cabinet for accessing what's in the drawers.

  Lateral files are 18 inches deep and vary in width from 24–48 inches and come in a range of heights. They are useful when there is plenty of wall space, and two-drawer styles can double as credenzas.

- **Storage of Frequently Used Items.** For the purposes of office layout, the items you need to consider here are ones you need to have at your fingertips on any given day. This may be letterhead stationery or storage of products you send out regularly. Where is the best place to store these items, and what kind of space must you allow for them?

- **Shelves.** Every home office needs shelves, whether they are for reference books or work materials. If you already have some books or supplies that belong on shelves, you can measure what you're currently storing to get an idea of what you would need to provide in a new home office.

- **Display Area.** If you have products that are necessary for sales demonstrations, or if you're very proud of what you've accomplished, you'll need to allot space for displaying your work.

- **Visitor Seating.** If you plan to have clients or patients visit your office, you need to consider how you'll accommodate them. A chair next to the desk or on the opposite side of the desk is one option. Another choice, space permitting, is to have a couch or armchair arrangement where you can both talk to each other across a coffee table.

- **Employee Work Area or Visitor Waiting Area.** If you have employees, you may want a separate work area for them. Most people find it very distracting to have someone else around full-time, particularly if both of you must make phone calls. Try to arrange for any employees to have work space that is separate from yours.

And while any client you're seeing will, of course, be ushered into your office, consider where they'll wait when you can't see them immediately. (If the visitor waiting area is in close proximity to your office, a sound machine in the waiting area can help cover any conversations they might overhear.)

WHAT YOU NEED WHERE: A CHECKLIST

Use the checklist on the opposite page as a guideline. (The "Elsewhere" column is to note items you'll want or need but that should be located elsewhere in the house; the "Not needed" column demarcates items that are not necessary for you to work at home.)

KEEP IT SIMPLE

1. Choose your desk carefully based on where you plan to put your computer, how much surface space you want, and what type of drawers are practical for your work.

	In office	Elsewhere	Not needed
Desk	/ /	/ /	/ /
Computer table	/ /	/ /	/ /
Worktable or conference table	/ /	/ /	/ /
Special equipment (copier, fax, scanner, etc.) List and note what you'll need			
_____	/ /	/ /	/ /
_____	/ /	/ /	/ /
_____	/ /	/ /	/ /
_____	/ /	/ /	/ /
_____	/ /	/ /	/ /
File cabinets	/ /	/ /	/ /
Storage space	/ /	/ /	/ /
Shelving	/ /	/ /	/ /
Display area	/ /	/ /	/ /
Visitor seating	/ /	/ /	/ /
Waiting area	/ /	/ /	/ /

2. If space is at a premium, consider what office items you could place elsewhere in the house.

3. List all the other furniture, equipment, or special areas (visitor waiting area?) and plan accordingly.

5
CREATING A
COMFORTABLE
LAYOUT

WHAT'S AHEAD

Consider Work Flow

Do-It-Yourself Design

Planning Where Everything Goes

Wall Layout

Noise and Lighting

Helpful Hints

If you're already using the space as an office but are dissatisfied with how it's working, forget all your current habits and try to evaluate the room with a fresh eye. Now is the time to keep what has worked in the past but take a new look at aspects of the room that no longer work well.

CONSIDER WORK FLOW

- Work flow is the key to any office layout.
    - —To what equipment and furniture do you need access?
    - —What is your work or work style? Papers spread out? Working from detailed lists? Accounting? Drafting?
    - —Do you need to stand to do any of the tasks?
    - —Are you at the computer full-time or only occasionally?
    - —Are you on the phone full-time or only occasionally?
    - —Do you need to plan for others regularly coming in and out of your office?

DO-IT-YOURSELF DESIGN

If you have some type of home design software program, then planning your office layout can be done on the computer. If not, pencil, scissors, and graph paper will provide you with a quick-and-easy way to come up with a good room scheme.

- Take a piece of graph paper and sketch out the room's dimensions, letting each square represent one foot of actual floor space. Note the position of windows, doors, closets, radiators, heating vents, changes in elevation, and mark on the sketch the current placement of phone jacks and electrical outlets.

- Use cut-outs to represent furniture and equipment. Measure the dimensions of all furniture and equipment you plan to use, and cut them out of a separate piece of graph paper, using the same one square to one foot scale. By creating furniture pieces you can move around easily, you can experiment with different layouts without having to erase anything—or without doing any heavy lifting of the furniture itself.

PLANNING WHERE EVERYTHING GOES

- Place your desk first. It's the most important piece of furniture in the office. Consider which way you want to face. Some find looking out a window or facing the door distracting; others find that they like to have a sense of the rest of the world.

- In general, office/desk layouts fall into three categories:

1. **Parallel layout.** Your desk forms one line, and a table or low storage piece sits right behind it, providing another surface you can reach easily from your chair.

2. **An L layout.** Often used to make the most of corners, an L can also be freestanding in the middle of a large room. The L configuration offers excellent access between desk surface and computer.

3. **Semicircle layout.** The desk and equipment encircle you on one side, providing easy access to all counter space.

Once you have on paper what you consider a comfortable desk layout, ask someone to come and help you move your furniture into place. Before making any permanent changes, it's a good idea to give the office a dress rehearsal.

WALL LAYOUT

- If you need your walls for major storage or display, measure the wall just as you did the room size and create a wall layout as well.

- If you need or want storage units or shelves, estimate how many you'd like to have and then consider the best place for them to be.

- If you have space to run shelves or storage from floor to ceiling, take advantage of it. Most home office owners will say that you can never have too much storage.

- Be careful when placing units at shoulder height and above. They can fit nicely above a desk or credenza but can be a liability if there is no furniture below—people are less likely to see something up high and may bump into them.

NOISE AND LIGHTING

No matter how carefully you've chosen your space, there are likely to be a few things wrong with it, and noise and lighting are two of the issues that are easier to solve in advance than later on.

Keeping down the noise:

- Carpet with a good quality padding underneath is an excellent sound absorber. Cushioned vinyl or rubber tile will also help create a quiet environment. Hardwood floors and ceramic tiles can make any noise reverberate.

- Outside noises can be buffered somewhat by draperies.

- Solid core doors rather than hollow ones should be used, and weather stripping on both doors and windows will help.

- Wall coverings such as fabric or cork will help absorb some sounds and having padded furniture in the room will also deaden noises. For true soundproofing, talk to a contractor about putting up acoustical drywall with thick insulation in between the walls.

- If sound is coming through a heat or air vent, your best bet is a low-playing CD player, a fish tank with an air pump, or "white noise" generator.

Good lighting is key to a good work environment:

Consider the lighting of the space you've chosen. Windows will bring in warmth and sunlight, but they'll also bring in glare.

Every office can benefit from three types of light. The best offices have some natural light during part of the day. *Natural light* provides a cheerful freshness to the atmosphere that is difficult to duplicate any other way. It's also the least tiring and provides the truest color. *Ambient light*—light that spreads throughout the room—is also key to a good work environment. *Task lighting*—lighting that illuminates exactly what you're working on—is the third type of light you need in your office.

The older you are, the more seriously you'll consider lighting issues. As we age, our vision requires the aid of an increasing amount of light. Here are a few suggestions as you select the type of light you want:

- Keep your walls and ceilings a light color in order to maximize the light.

- Create a level of consistency in room lighting. Your eyes become fatigued if you have to constantly readjust to different light levels.

- Depending on the location of your office, consider adding a skylight. It's an excellent way to bring in additional light.

- Fluorescent lights are inexpensive and energy-efficient, but the light is diffused and the blinking of the light is irritating to some.

- Halogen bulbs create excellent task lighting—bright and clear. Halogens burn very hot, and pole lamps with halogen bulbs have been the cause of fires. If you decide to use halogens, talk to the lighting store or your electrician about how you plan to use them. Desk lamps with firm bases and high-hat ceiling fixtures with halogens, which can be used for task lighting, have been used successfully in many home offices.

- Chromalux bulbs provide a clear light that heightens contrast and makes it easier to see.

- To minimize desk clutter, look for a desk lamp that doesn't have to be in your way. Several styles feature a firm base or clamp for the edge of the desk. The light itself is on a long arm that can easily be positioned to light the center of your work space.

- Position your computer screen so that you're not looking directly at the screen with the window behind. You also don't want the sun shining onto your computer screen. Both situations are very tiring for the eyes.

HELPFUL HINTS

- Before settling into your office, call an electrician. You'll want a dedicated line for your computer, and you'll likely need outlets for some of your other equipment.

- Contact the phone company if necessary for additional modem or telephone lines.

- Install smoke alarms and purchase a fire extinguisher to keep handy.

- If you can afford it, get the office painted before you settle in. Once you're set up, you'll dread the day when you might have to make time for getting the place painted. While light colors will help make the office seem well lit, don't be afraid to have fun with the colors. There's no need for a home office to be sterile or boring in its decor. As a matter of fact, adding some personality to it through decoration will make going to work more fun.

- When choosing window coverings, keep in mind the practical—sound buffering, if needed, and light reduction—but select something you like that will add some character to the room.

- A few photos or mementos placed around the room are homey touches, but be careful of clutter. If you have lots of things you'd like to display, rotate them.

KEEP IT SIMPLE

1. When laying out your office, place your desk first, and put it where you'll have access to the storage and the equipment you'll use every day.

2. Develop a lighting plan that provides consistent lighting throughout your office. Eyes become fatigued when they have to keep readjusting to different light levels.

3. Paint the office before you move everything into it. If you use your home office regularly, you'll appreciate a nice paint job.

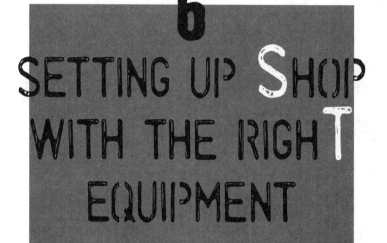

6
SETTING UP SHOP WITH THE RIGHT EQUIPMENT

WHAT'S AHEAD

Your Computer
Save Time
Protect Your Equipment
Trouble-Shooting
The Notebook Computer
The Fax Machine and Copier

Technology is changing so rapidly that the best advice I can offer you about "setting up shop" with your equipment is to stay informed about new developments in computers, copiers, and fax machines. The equipment is getting better and better, and prices are continually dropping, so replacing outmoded pieces may not be as expensive as you might think.

YOUR COMPUTER

- When shopping for a computer:

  —Purchase the most recent, most powerful model that has the features you need.

  —Opt for a machine with a large memory. You'll want a hard drive with enough space to be able to handle all the programs that you'll want for your computer.

  —Be sure to get a machine with a high-speed modem. Unless you have a cable connection or a high-speed ISDN line installed, you'll soon find that waiting on the Internet is hard to do. (Use a separate phone line for the modem.)

  —Ask about technical support. Some companies will ship replacement parts overnight.

SAVE TIME

- If there are aspects to your computer you don't understand, hire someone to teach you. You'll waste both time and money trying to figure out programs on your own, and you'll be more efficient if you know how to maximize use of your computer.

- Set up a logical filing system on your computer with meaningful names so that you'll know what you have.

- Think carefully before installing games on your office computer. If you're prone to procrastination, resist the temptation to play by not installing any games.

PROTECT YOUR EQUIPMENT

- Use a surge protector.

- Once you start going online you run the risk of picking up a virus, so having an antivirus program is vital to keep your equipment running. If you ever swap disks with anyone, be sure to do an antivirus scan of the disk before you open any files.

- Install a backup program. Computer experts say it's not "if"

.your computer will crash, it's "when," so don't become lazy. Keep backing up. To be fully covered, establish this system:

1. Once a month make a complete backup of your hard drive using the tape backup system, and save this copy until you make another full copy at the end of the month. This copy should be kept off the premises. Send it to your spouse's office or any place where you'd have access to it in case of a household fire.

2. A full backup should also be done from week to week so that in case of a crash you have a reasonably up-to-date backup. (The monthly backup offers greater protection against viruses; if you were to have to rebuild your data, the older backup might be virus-free even if the weekly backup isn't.)

3. On a nightly basis, evaluate whether or not you've done work that you'd hate to have to recreate if anything were to happen before the next day. If so, copy those files onto a diskette.

- If you think you'll never remember to back up regularly, investigate how to program your system so it does so automatically. Then you never have to think about it.

TROUBLE-SHOOTING

- If you're a telecommuter, put the number of your tech support staff in your address book. Make certain you have more than one number in case that line is busy or the person is out.

- If you're not a telecommuter and don't have access to a tech support team, make note of the technical support numbers of your software and hardware vendors.

- And unless you're a computer whiz yourself (or related to one), find yourself a computer "wizard." If someone helped you install the computer, that person is generally very savvy about how they work. Ask if you can hire him or her on an as-needed basis if something goes wrong.

- Invest in tech support "insurance" by paying to have a "support service agreement" with an independent company. Through the Internet you can find 24-hour technical support companies that supply immediate telephone support for many of the major software applications. They will work with you until a specific incident is resolved. If you should need them, you won't begrudge ever having had to pay an initial fee.

- If something does go wrong, make a note in your Office Notebook (see Chapter 8) about any error messages that are appearing on the screen and think back to anything that has been installed recently. Adding a program or downloading from the Internet can sometimes change the basic configuration of what you have. The person who is diagnosing the problem will need to know these things.

- Unless your computer is totally down, try to wait until afternoon to call a tech support number. They'll have more time to spend with you. Mornings, particularly Monday mornings, can be a harried time for the staff. Don't be irritable (it's not the technician's fault you're having a problem), and do listen to what he or she says. Sometimes people get so rattled they're unable to do what is suggested, which makes the problem much more difficult to fix.

- If you fail to get help right away, post your problem on the technical bulletin board of an online service. You may get just the answer you need.

- Make it a priority to keep learning about your computer. If something goes wrong, the telephone tech support person may want to talk you through fixing it. The more you understand about your computer, the greater the likelihood that you'll be able to get yourself up and running again with this type of help.

- Store the manuals for your software and hardware in an accessible place so that you can find them quickly if something goes wrong. Also store your software diskettes in this location in case you ever have to reload a program.

THE NOTEBOOK COMPUTER

These portable computers are getting lighter and cheaper with time:

- Shop for one that is lightweight and comfortable to use.

- Check the screen to make certain that the resolution is good.

- Test out each model's version of a "mouse." Some people like the touch pads; others like the central pointing sticks. See what's most comfortable for you.

- If you travel a great deal, carry a spare battery pack.

- If you're using a palm-size computer for your day planner, consider whether adding a normal-size keyboard will accomplish what you need.

THE FAX MACHINE AND COPIER

Older fax machines used to be less expensive if you settled for thermal paper. Today you can pick up a plain paper fax that functions as printer, scanner, and copier as well, so the improvements in technology will serve you well.

- Make certain the fax has the features you need. Many have several speed-dial positions, most have memory (so that an incoming fax can be stored if you are low on ink or out of paper), and most have a broadcast feature that permits you to send one fax to several different numbers.

- If you buy an all-in-one unit, make certain you're not compromising on any piece of equipment you really need.

- If your copying needs are for a letter here and there, then your fax machine will be just perfect. Major copying jobs should be taken to an outside service. If, however, you regularly need to do a lot of copying, then you may want to invest in a regular copier. Check the Yellow Pages under "photocopy machines" and talk to several sales reps. Most sell new machines as well as reconditioned ones. Look for a fast unit, and you may want one that sorts and collates, though those additional accessories do begin to run up the price.

- You'll want a service contract (the expense of any replacement parts is so high that it's foolish to run the risk of having to pay it), so that whether it's a new or reconditioned model doesn't matter—they've got to stand behind their product.

- Like junk mail, there are junk faxes. If you start receiving these, your best recourse is to fax back to the offending machine requesting that your number be removed from the list.

KEEP IT SIMPLE

1. Invest in the most powerful computer with the largest memory that you can afford. This will make it easier to update.

2. Store manuals, diskettes, and tech support numbers somewhere accessible where you can get your hands on them in a hurry.

3. When it comes to your computer, back up, back up, back up.

PART THREE

MANAGING

TIME

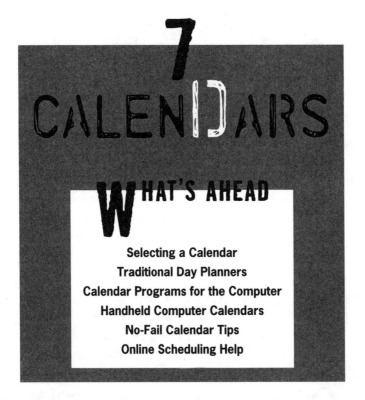

7
CALENDARS

WHAT'S AHEAD

Selecting a Calendar
Traditional Day Planners
Calendar Programs for the Computer
Handheld Computer Calendars
No-Fail Calendar Tips
Online Scheduling Help

The single most important tool for getting organized in business is your calendar, yet I constantly see all types of calendar abuse:

—Planners with coffee cup stains are more common than flowers in springtime.

—Calendars hide under stacks of paper as if they weren't meant to be seen.

—Multiple planners devoted to multiple facets of a single personality (guaranteed to produce schizophrenia).

—Computer calendars purchased with the best of intentions that sit unused because the owners haven't learned the system.

"Calendar Ridiculous" is the only way to describe the habits of a friend of mine who has the worst system I've ever seen, with multiple calendars she often forgets to use. As a result, she gets to the right place at the wrong time or the wrong place at the right time—providing she remembers where she is supposed to be at all; she frequently can't read what she's written!

Among her calendars is an amazing one she carries with her—it's one of the largest, fattest planners in existence (one designed to be left on a desk). At any given time it's stuffed with a minimum of fifty pieces of paper: notes, lists, directions, clipped items to read, business cards, invitations—more or less her entire life. The last time we got together for lunch she arrived thirty-five minutes late, huffing and puffing. She'd lost the address, and since she couldn't remember the correct name of the restaurant, she wasn't able to call. I smiled gently and suggested that there was a better way to manage her life. "But it will take too much time to set up a new system," she answered.

I thought to myself, But look at how much time you've already lost because your current system of choice is totally unmanageable!

Now that you're on your own, there's no one to notice if you forget to write something down, and no one to remind you of a meeting—you're on your own now. You have to carefully manage your time and find a calendar that will help you remain true to your schedule and your priorities.

Before you get started, I want you to make special note of these three calendar rules:

Rule 1: Use only one calendar. If you've formerly had one for personal scheduling and another for the office, now it's time to have everything in one place.

Rule 2: Write down everything. Even your "standing" appointments that "you'll never forget." Why? Because one day you will.

Rule 3: Check your calendar every day. (That's why you can't keep it under a stack of papers.) You would be surprised at the number of people who forget appointments and then explain: "I had it written down—I just forgot to look at my calendar!"

SELECTING A CALENDAR

Whether you opt for a palmtop computer calendar, a computer program calendar, or a paper-based system, the important thing to keep in mind is that a good calendar must function as a complete scheduling companion, with enough room for information about your appointments, space for a daily "to do" list, a way to view the weeks ahead, and a telephone directory. In addition, most people want a diary section for work accomplished and a place to keep track of business expenses.

TRADITIONAL DAY PLANNERS

In paper calendars or day planners, I like the styles that have a one- or two-page spread for each day so that there's plenty of room to keep track of what you're doing. Some very good models are no bigger than 4 by 7 inches, making them highly portable, too.

When choosing a day planner/calendar, consider:

- Is it portable? Some are quite bulky and heavy.
- Does it have adequate space to keep track of your daily schedule as well as the weeks ahead?
- Is there a section for "to do" lists, checklists, and a section for notes?
- Is there space for expenses?
- Is there an area for recording your car mileage?
- Is there a telephone directory?
- Are there places for a pen, your train schedule, etc., and other things you need to carry with you?

CALENDAR PROGRAMS FOR THE COMPUTER

Some people opt for the computer-based calendars. They like the carryover of information without having to rewrite it the way you must with paper calendars. The integrated address book, "to do" list, date book, e-mail, and reminder systems are also an asset. While you can always generate a paper printout, remember that if you're away from your computer for long periods of time, this system may not be the one for you. The benefits of the computer program are largely what you gain by having it handy a good part of the time.

When shopping for a computer program calendar:

- Tell the salesperson what model of paper calendar you've been using. Many of the traditional day planners have computer counterparts so you can simply pick up the software version of what you've been using.

- Plan to carry a printout. Because your calendar won't be portable, you'll need to get in the habit of creating something that is.

HANDHELD COMPUTER CALENDARS

In electronic handheld models, the world is going to be overtaken by the palmtop computer calendars. While less elaborate electronic versions used to be a serious option, the fact that these palmtops are highly portable but also interface with your own computer make them a very attractive choice. (Some interface with fax machines and online services, and more models will soon offer these options.) While data can be input directly into the palmtop computer, the fact that you can connect it to your computer and do most of the input on a large keyboard makes a huge difference in convenience. Users can also create a paper printout from the larger computer, and so this overcomes the need to be totally reliant on the palmtop. You can carry the printout with you as a calendar or make extra copies to leave with staff or family members as well.

When shopping for a palmtop:

- Be certain your computer and the palmtop are compatible.

- Check the screen. Can you read it easily? Those that are back-lit seem to be most adaptable to a variety of conditions.

- How is information entered? If your hands are big you may be uncomfortable with using some of the small keyboards.

- Evaluate size and weight to make certain you'll be comfortable carrying it.

- If you travel a good deal and will need to hook up while away, you may need to buy a snap-on modem. This will permit you to download and send e-mail from the road.

- Ask about backing up your data—the single most important quality of any type of electronic computer. If you lose what you've entered and have no backup, you'll waste a great deal of time and angst trying to restore it.

NO-FAIL CALENDAR TIPS

- Write top priority items in red ink.

- When you book an appointment or a meeting, write down the name, address, and telephone number of where you're going. If you need directions for getting there, write them down next to the appointment (creating a permanent record). If space doesn't allow, write the directions on a separate piece of paper, and note in your calendar where you're filing them (your Tickler file or the file with the information for the meeting would both be ideal places).

- Use your calendar to reduce paper. Toss invitations after you've entered the necessary information; don't hang on to slips regarding dental appointments once you've entered the date, time, and place.

- You can further reduce clutter by noting on your calendar the details of *possible* events you might like to attend. (This is a better reminder system than keeping a flier or an ad for an event floating around your desk.) When the day arrives you can make a decision about whether or not you have time to go.

- Review your activities a week in advance so that you can plan around your existing appointments.

- Sit down with your calendar each evening, and review what you need to do the next day. Write everything down.

- Use your calendar to keep track of your daily "to do" list (see Chapter 8).

- Make appointments with yourself for "Priority Time" when you plan to work on a specific project.

- If you're having difficulty reaching someone, set up a telephone appointment and write it down just as you would a regular appointment.

- Most calendar systems today have an area for annotating what work was accomplished each day—use it. This type of accounting is particularly important for the telecommuter and the self-employed because it answers the question, "Where did my time go?" Once you've observed what's taking up your time, you're better prepared to manage it.

ONLINE SCHEDULING HELP

There are now Internet services that function as personal calendars. The sites are private, password-protected, and feature online calendars where you can enter your daily schedule. If you travel a great deal, you no longer need to be concerned about carrying your calendar with you since—assuming you have access to an Internet hookup—you can reach your personal schedule from anywhere. In addition, you can give access to co-workers who might need to check your schedule. One site also offers a lengthy listing of events: meetings and trade shows, movie and video releases, Web events, book releases, upcoming television shows, and financial events. With a click of your mouse you can add any event that interests you to your personal calendar, making your calendar a combination of personal information and professional events you learned about through the site.

KEEP IT SIMPLE

1. Select the calendar style that's right for you and use only that one calendar.

2. Plan out your day the night before. Write down all appointments and record a complete "to do" list.

3. Be sure to check your calendar daily!

8

YOUR KEY TO ORGANIZATION:

THE MASTER LIST/ OFFICE NOTEBOOK

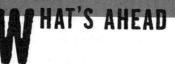

WHAT'S AHEAD

The Master List/Office Notebook
Preparing Your Daily "To Do" List
Tips for Using Your List Well

I visit countless offices where I find executives keeping track of things on lists they keep everywhere. I follow them to meetings where I see them make notes on scraps of paper or in the margin of the agenda; and I consult with them at their desks where they show me notes they've written on backs of everything (letters, file folders, business reports, and envelopes as well as more acceptable legal pads). Most people are all too happy to write it down—they start one list only to find another, until with exasperation they announce, "I know I wrote it down here somewhere!"

The system I recommend involves creating a Master List in a spiral notebook, which will now be known as your Office Notebook. It will be from here that you cull your daily "to do" list. Today many people like keeping their Master List on their palmtop computer or within the scheduling software of their regular computer. I think this is an excellent way to keep track of your "to do" list—just the way most people write that information on a calendar or a daily planner. However, I still recommend a paper-based system for your Master List. All your notes and tasks to do can be viewed easily, and because the information is chronological, you can look back to trace anything you need.

Another well-kept "secret" about the Office Notebook is that keeping one is a guaranteed way to manage all the items on which you need to follow up. Why remember that you need to purchase that new software magazine, or that you're to be receiving a document you need from a client in a week? These are the types of things you can note in your Office Notebook and be reminded of in such a way that you can take action when appropriate.

THE MASTER LIST/OFFICE NOTEBOOK

- If you opt for a paper-based system, buy a spiral notebook; lefties may prefer a steno pad so the spirals are on the top.

- Each day, note the date on top of the page. As you note things to do and phone calls to make and those completed, you'll begin to create a "history" of your work life. Because items are recorded by date, even miscellaneous items are easy enough to find.

- Get in the habit of writing *everything* down—from "buy stamps" to "start XYZ Project," every item that needs to be done should be a part of this running list.

- Mark priority items with an asterisk.

- Break big projects into "action steps."

- Note a "finish by" date for those items with a known deadline; for example, "prepare agenda for conference; to be mailed out by 2/22." Make note of the final date by which the agenda must be completed, and mark it on your calendar so that you have a backup system.

- Always note in your Master List the basics of the information you need. If you're to call someone, note the telephone number; if you're to mail them something, write down the address. Periodically, or at the time when you're ready to "retire" this Master List notebook, go through the entire list and transfer any names, addresses, or phone numbers that should be added to your address book. If you're working with a list on your computer, this can be as simple as "drag and drop."

- All papers related to projects on the Master List belong in appropriate files. I visit far too many offices where the inhabitants use stacks of papers as a "reminder list." Now all those stacks can be filed, with only the running list on your desk.

PREPARING YOUR DAILY "TO DO" LIST

- Set aside ten minutes at the end of each day to prepare a "to do" list for the next day.
- Review any undone items from that day's list and carry them over if necessary.
- Look at your schedule for the upcoming day, and select any additional items from your Master List that you might be able to accomplish. If you have an appointment near the library, you might select that day to visit the library to do needed research.
- Place a star by the items that are most important. If something unexpected occurs during the day, you can quickly focus

on those items that should take priority if you do have the time.

- Don't overschedule. Plan no more than 75 percent of the day so you'll have time to cope with interruptions and other unexpected problems.

- At the end of each day, update your Master List by crossing off the items you have finished. Also note down any new tasks that have come to mind.

TIPS FOR USING YOUR LIST WELL

- Your Master List notes: "Follow up with P. Smith regarding the new equipment purchase." You call Paula Smith only to learn that she's out of town for three days. You can leave a message, but you want to be certain you stay on top of this. Skip forward in your calendar four days (to give her time to return to her office) and note that you need to call her again. When you phone on the fourth day, you learn that she is now in the Far East for three weeks. No sense leaving a phone message now. How to remember to follow up in three weeks? Drop a reminder note in your Tickler file in the folder for the following month. In the meantime, the "Call P. Smith regarding the equipment purchase" item remains on your Master

List as a surefire reminder that you still need to take care of that task.

- Unless you carry either your "to do" list or your Master List with you constantly, then you need to create a method for making notes when you don't have either one with you. Many people carry a "jotter," a small notepad; others prefer index cards or make notes in their calendars. What you use makes little difference, you just want to make sure you add them to your Master List when you get home.

- Keep pen and paper in logical places so that you're sure to write things down: by your bedside, in your car (purchase an "autopad" with pencil attached); by all telephones; in your briefcase. Make notes when you think of them and then add them to your Master List once you're back in your office. If you don't make this transfer, then you're back to where you began—having lists and lists and more lists.

- Leave messages for yourself on voice mail if you're away and are afraid you'll forget.

KEEP IT SIMPLE

1. Record all "to do" items on one Master List. Your daily "to do" list will be culled from this running list.

2. Mark priority items with an asterisk and note due dates for projects that have them.

3. Set aside ten minutes at the end of your day to plan your next day's "to do" list. Schedule only 75 percent of your day so that you can cope with the unexpected.

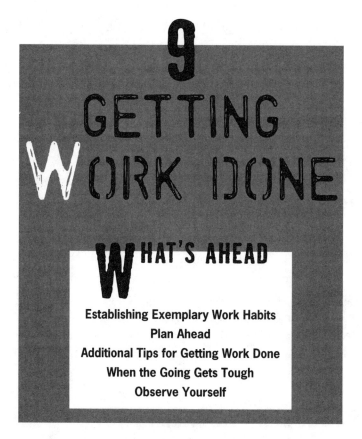

9
GETTING
WORK DONE

WHAT'S AHEAD

Establishing Exemplary Work Habits
Plan Ahead
Additional Tips for Getting Work Done
When the Going Gets Tough
Observe Yourself

Getting business work done at home is very different from getting work done at the office. A certain level of purpose and discipline seems to fill the air when you're in a "real" office environment. At home, there are no rules or expectations being filtered down from the top—you're the top—and it's more challenging to achieve that same level of drive and discipline. There is so much flexibility and so many options to consider that it actually creates problems; if the interruptions don't weaken you, the distractions will: "Should I do my errands first thing and then settle down to work, or should I work first?" "Should I work through lunch and quit early, or should I take a walk at lunchtime and put in another four or five hours?" And of course, there are the dilemmas posed by having a family: "If I take time off to go to Jan's softball game, will I really be able to make up for it on Saturday?"

What's more, there's still gender bias. The man working at home is "really working" and mustn't be disturbed. On the other hand, a woman is still expected to be "on call" and wear many hats by fitting in daytime volunteer work and squeezing in extra errands around her work schedule, not to mention solving problems, lending a hand, and keeping the home running smoothly in her "free time."

Nonetheless, it is entirely possible to be extremely productive working from home, and it starts with basic habits and a clear mindset.

ESTABLISHING EXEMPLARY WORK HABITS

Getting work done takes focus and discipline, and once you've established a pattern that works for you, it needs to be repeated over and over again to become fully engrained as part of who you are. The best gift you can give yourself is to create a regular structure for your work schedule—you don't have to start work at the exact same moment every day, but you do need to establish that once you arrive at your desk you immediately start working on what needs to be done. Here are some simple ways to put better work habits in motion:

- Hit the ground running. The easiest way to do this is to be certain to conclude each work session by taking time to create a "to do" list for the next day. When you arrive at your desk the next morning, you know exactly what it is you need to do. (See Chapter 8 for information on "to do" lists.)

- Set achievable goals. Don't put twenty items on your daily "to do" list. Calculate what you can realistically get done and write down only those items. Leave everything else on your master list in your Office Notebook for another day. (See Chapter 8.)

- Maximize your "prime time." There's been a lot written about identifying whether you're a lark or an owl, but when it comes to getting things done, it's important to know your preferences. If you really don't get going until 11:00 A.M., then start your morning with filing, answering correspondence, and returning some phone calls. If, however, morning is your prime time, then get started on your major task of the day. Screen calls and devote a specific amount of time to getting your most difficult work done. Your afternoon can be reserved for work that's less challenging.

- View projects as a series of steps rather than one big project. That way you'll know exactly what you're doing and what comes next.

- Allow more time than you expect for a project. That way you haven't shortchanged yourself on time to devote to the task, and if you do finish more quickly than you expected, then the bonus time is all yours!

- Make appointments with yourself. If you have a major project, then set aside time for it. Note the "appointment" on your calendar: "9 A.M.: work on ABC account."

PLAN AHEAD

- Anticipate. Think through the work materials you'll need for a particular project and have them nearby when you start working. That way you don't need to keep hopping up and down to get things.

- Also anticipate family needs. If you drive the carpool on Tuesday afternoons, and a client schedules a big group meeting you need to attend for Tuesday, make other arrangements for the carpool as soon as you learn of the conflict.

- Learn to say no. You know you can't do everything. Tell people that now so you don't get in over your head later on.

- If you have recurring paperwork, establish a specific time to do it once a week. Note it on your calendar. By making it routine, you'll find the tasks easier to do.

- Cluster "like" projects. Group your phone calls. Set aside one time to handle the mail or pay bills.

- In your Office Notebook, keep a list of "when I have the time" items. Work at fitting these items into time slots during the day; if you have projects in mind, you'll be surprised at how many opportunities you'll have for getting small things done.

- Always carry something to do. Whether you're waiting in the world's longest line at the post office or stuck at an airport with a delayed flight, if you have work or reading to do, you'll find the time can be used quite productively.

ADDITIONAL TIPS FOR GETTING WORK DONE

- Leave the house. Sometimes the best way to get concentrated work done is by going to a different environment where there are no distractions.

- Delegate. If you have a staff then you have an obvious person to whom to delegate. If you don't, you need to be more creative. Think through your office tasks and consider what could be handled by an outside service or a "temp" who could come in for a short time. Also consider what home chores might be delegated. If your youngest child has now started kindergarten, perhaps your baby-sitter would be willing to absorb a few more household tasks to free you for more work time.

- Set interim goals.

- Set definite deadlines for things and tell someone what they are. The items on which people most often procrastinate are tasks where there's no definite deadline.

- Don't let unpleasant tasks build up.

- Vary your pace. After a tough job, plan to do a few menial ones in between.

- Keep up with day-to-day items. Set a kitchen timer for 15 minutes and dive into your filing or some of your day-to-day paperwork to begin getting things done.

- Use small chunks of time. Too often people keep waiting for that big block of time to undertake that overwhelmingly large project. The only problem is that we seldom get big chunks of time, so that big project just sits there until panic sets in.

- Give yourself one enjoyable task to look forward to each day.

- Once you begin a project, stick with it. Even if you're interrupted, don't use that as an opportunity to stop work. Too often people flit from task to task, never having the satisfaction of completing any one thing. (See Chapter 11 for ideas on coping with interruptions.)

- Try to finish one task before starting the next one. While this isn't always possible because you have to wait for approvals or to hear back from someone, the important thing to keep in mind is that many "open" projects just lead to feeling overwhelmed.

- Force yourself to make minor decisions quickly. Our lives today are just too fast-paced to let things linger if we don't need to.

- Streamline any task that you can. Create one basic "sales" letter and use it as your master for all other letters, making adjustments only as needed. Set up computer-generated mailing lists so that future mailings can be sent out quickly and easily.

- Keep asking, Is this the simplest way to do it? As you begin to understand a project, you may come up with ways to save yourself time.

- Recognize progress and establish small rewards during large projects.

- Improve your working conditions. If your desk is messy or you've got music playing in the background, these things may be serving to distract you.

- Use leisure time for leisure. You'll be surprised at how this helps.

WHEN THE GOING GETS TOUGH

- Bargain with yourself. Tell yourself you won't get up from the desk until you've done what you've been putting off. People find it exhilarating to no longer have that nagging feeling in the back of their mind.

- Make an arbitrary start. Sometimes certain projects aren't clear when we first start out; try making an "opening move" so that you have a better feel for the project and can now stipulate action steps.

- Keep going. Remember, a first draft or a beginning step is merely one of many documents on the way to something that's well written or well done.

- When you're stuck or aren't working productively, take a break. Get up from your desk, leave your office, go on a walk or to the kitchen to have a cup of coffee. Set a time limit for your break, perhaps 15–30 minutes. By stepping away for a few minutes, your stress level will subside, and you'll find when you return you'll feel refreshed and can make a new start.

OBSERVE YOURSELF

- Periodically assess your own management of time. Check your desk for clutter and consider whether or not you've been getting things done satisfactorily. Have you fallen into any bad habits? (Jumping up to check the fax machine whenever you hear a fax coming through? Stopping to read the mail when it arrives at 11:30 A.M. instead of waiting until you planned to do it?)

- Create a time log of your day to see where you're investing your time.

- Keep track of how long projects take. This will help you gauge what to work on, partially based on the time available to you on any given day.

- Record how much time you spend on the telephone, who initiates the call, and how quickly you can bring a conversation to conclusion.

- When you're delaying on something, evaluate why. This will help you overcome what's bothering you, and, ultimately, you'll be able to get the job done.

K EEP IT SIMPLE

1. Establish a regular structure to your work pattern in order to better manage your time.

2. View projects as a series of steps, and identify exactly what it is you need to get done on any given day.

3. Don't wait for a big block of time in which to get work done. Start using small chunks of time, and you'll be surprised at what you can accomplish in 5-, 15-, and 30-minute blocks of time.

10
THE TELEPHONE

WHAT'S AHEAD

Making Basic Decisions

Ideal Telephone Features for a Home Office

Cellular Phones

Pagers

Telephone Answering Devices

Technological Advances

Outgoing Calls

Incoming Calls

Ending a Call

Recording Your Outgoing Message

Returning Calls

Telephone Directories

Time-Savers

W hile telephones aren't yet at the Dick Tracy video-wristwatch-communicator stage, we're not that far away from it, either. Telephones today have amazing features that can almost replace the need for an assistant in a home office.

I know from years of helping people set up home offices that there are two important points in making efficient use of the telephone:

1. **A telephone system** (including answering devices and pagers) that has the "bells and whistles" you need.
2. **Personal habits** that help you manage the phone efficiently.
    This chapter will explain both.

M AKING BASIC DECISIONS

With today's heavy reliance on technological methods of keeping in touch (pagers, modems, and faxes, in addition to regular phones), it's important to carefully consider several issues that will affect your basic system. And by making these decisions now, you'll have a better idea what services you want to have priced when you talk to competing telephone service companies.

How many lines do you need? For an actively used home office, I strongly recommend that you have *at least* three lines coming into your home: one line should be for home use, the second should be your business line, and the third should be dedicated to the computer modem and fax. Why so many? Because anything less is just not sufficient. Haven't you called homes where their phone line is totally blocked for an hour or more because someone in the family is online?

With separate lines for home and business, you can "close" the office nights and weekends by letting an answering device cover that line; it also lets youngsters answer the home line but keeps them off the business one. (Consider having that line only in your office; that way your kids won't ever make a mistake.)

Another advantage to having a true business line is that it offers you a listing in the business directory, and some telephone companies let you code calls. This can be handy when it comes to passing charges on to clients.

Do you need a toll-free number for incoming calls? If customers are calling you to place orders or for information, you'll increase the number of calls you get if you have a toll-free number. (By deciding now, you'll have a better idea what services you want priced by competing telephone services.)

Do you want Call Waiting? This service can be a great convenience (you don't miss a call) *and* a great annoyance (important calls are interrupted by Call Waiting). Some companies offer an "override" feature to turn off this service before initiating or receiving certain calls. You don't worry about missing a call, though, because you can have a voice mail service take messages.

Do you need Call Forwarding? For a home office worker with no secretary or assistant, Call Forwarding provides you with the opportunity of having your calls follow you. An additional service available through some phone companies offers you the option of changing your forwarding instructions; if you're not touching bases at home, you can call in from another phone and change your forwarding instructions.

Do you want three-way calling? Three-way calling offers an easy way to have a conversation with more than one person. Conference calls can involve a greater number of people but they must be arranged by a phone company.

What about Caller ID? Caller ID can be a tremendous benefit to home-based workers. Consider this scenario: You're working on a major project and don't want to be interrupted; the phone rings—it may be the client with some new details . . . With Caller ID, you'll know in an instant whether or not to pick up the phone to talk to your client, or whether the incoming call will simply distract you from the work at hand. You can now opt for Caller ID with Name, which helps in identifying calls when you don't recognize the number.

Do you need a translation service? Some phone companies offer a translation service for businesspeople who have a lot of overseas business.

Consider the hours at which you do your phoning and whether the calls are local or long distance. Having this information when you speak to the companies about their services will be helpful.

If you've made these basic decisions, the telephone companies can be very helpful in offering suggestions and putting together some type of package price. Talk to your local provider as well as a long-distance provider to see what options you have. Compare prices of several different companies; one company may offer a significantly better package than another.

Once you're a customer, ask about setting up the service so that you can't be "slammed." This is when another provider switches your service to their company without your permission. This can cost you money, and it will definitely cost you time in straightening out who your service provider is supposed to be.

Every so often, check back with the companies to see what's new. A company may be offering a new "special" and may be able to save you additional money.

IDEAL TELEPHONE FEATURES FOR A HOME OFFICE

It's been a long time since home owners phoned one telephone company that then sent out a man—and it was a man—to hook up the phone service and deliver the number of black phones ordered. More recently, consumers have been offered the option of renting a telephone from the phone company or buying a unit of their own from a competitor. Most people with home offices will have greater satisfaction with the units they purchase themselves, and here are some of the features you may want to consider in an in-office telephone. (Cellular phones will be discussed next.)

Cordless phone. Cordless phones today offer more range and better quality than ever before. Home office workers who want to be able to wander around the office or walk to another part of the home while on the phone may find this an attractive option.

Priority ringing. With this option, you can change the sound of the ring—one ring can denote a business call, a ring with a different sound can indicate personal calls.

Speed dial and redial features. These are timesaving conveniences worth having. Speed dial stores regularly phoned numbers so that you can dial them by hitting one button or a couple of digits. Redial lets you hit one button to re-call a number that you've just called (from that unit only).

Hold button. An absolute must so that you can maneuver between lines in a businesslike manner. You can program some telephone systems to play music while the caller is on hold.

Mute button. Another must for anyone with a family or an audible pet—whether it's a baby crying, a dog barking, or a parrot squawking, it's good to be able to shield your callers from the personal aspects of your life.

Speakerphone. While speakerphones aren't ideal for prolonged discussions or private ones, they do keep your hands free while a number you've called is ringing or when you're placed on hold.

Headset. These are a great add-on, and some phones are even being sold with headsets. Ergonomically, a headset is much healthier for you than holding a phone to your ear or cradling a receiver between your shoulder and ear. A headset leaves your hands free throughout calls, and yet, unlike a speakerphone where people sometimes sound "like they're in barrels," the sound quality of the call is uncompromised.

Doorbell connection. The doorbell can be connected into some phone systems so that you can talk to the person at the front door by answering the phone. This can be a huge time-saver for the home-based worker: "Yes, I'm home, leave the package on the porch," or "No, I don't have time to see what you're selling today."

Phone with answering machine. You will want an answering device of some type, but before investing in a phone with a built-in machine, read some of the pros and cons in comparing answering machines with voice mail. (See the following page for more information.) It may affect your decision.

CELLULAR PHONES

To stay in touch today, most people want to have a cell phone. Prices have dropped considerably, and technology has improved immeasurably. Now you practically need a guidebook to decide what kind of cell phone to buy because the options offered are so varied. With certain cell phones, you can have everything from Caller ID and three-way calling to systems that receive e-mail and from which you can send faxes.

One type of wireless phone might best be termed a "mobile" phone. These can be installed directly into cars and purchased with features such as voice-activated dialing and speakerphone connections that aid in safer driving while talking. Other cellular phones are the kind that fit into your purse or breast pocket.

When it comes to choosing a cellular phone, your first and most basic decision concerns what you need its range to be. While digital services dominate the cellular phone industry, if you travel in remote areas, you may be better off with an analog system. A good salesperson will be able to tell you what type of phone will best suit your needs and explain to you any limits of the service area.

Once you've made this basic decision, here are some of the other issues to keep in mind.

Do you want or need a cell phone with a screen? The latest models have a small display that enables you to read e-mail, check appointments, play back voice mail messages, and even play games when you're bored.

How does the pricing structure work? Most service plans are based on a monthly charge for a set number of minutes. There may be a slightly higher charge for calls made during peak times. You also pay for incoming calls.

Are there "landline" charges for calling regular homes or offices? What about "roaming" charges (if you're outside the local area)? Is there an activation fee or a cancellation fee for a broken contract (which might happen if you get a new phone)? Don't be caught by surprise by these charges, and some companies charge more for certain types of calls, so check out anything that might be in the "fine print."

Ask about battery performance—talk life vs. standby life. You also want a low-charge alert function so you don't miss calls because your batteries died on you suddenly.

If you need to call customer service, what is the response time? Test this out before signing up with a provider.

What is the length of the contract? These services are changing all the time, and you may not want to sign up for an eternity.

Depending on their importance to you, here are other questions to ask: *Does the carrier offer voice or alphanumeric paging? How many numbers can be stored? Is there auto redial? Speed dial? Ringer select (different rings can mean different things to you)? Caller ID? Speed dial? Voice mail? E-mail retrieval? Fax option? Web access? And for how much? Is there an up-charge if you're out of the regular calling area?* If you're using the phone primarily in the car, you'll also want a holder for the car. Ask, too, for voice-activated dialing.

If you're a light cell phone user, here's a new option. Consider buying prepaid cell phone cards. On a per-minute basis, they are more expensive than many regular cellular service plans. However, if you own your own cell phone and use it infrequently, it makes a lot more sense to buy a phone card and pay as you need it rather than having to pay monthly for a service you may or may not use. Like other calling cards, cell phone cards are available at convenience stores. Some cards can be reloaded over the phone, or you can simply buy a new card when you need one.

PAGERS

Pagers are yet another way of staying in touch with people who need you. Having your cell phone ring while you're meeting with a client is a distraction to both of you, yet if your beeper is on "vibrate," you're still able to get the word that someone is trying to get in touch. Beepers make you available in an emergency, and they are perfect if you're usually near a telephone anyway—receive a beep and then return the call.

And like all other forms of technology, pagers are transforming themselves into digital wonders. Here are the three types of pagers you might consider—from the most basic to the more elaborate:

1. **A numeric beeper.** This is the oldest and simplest form of paging system, and it's perfectly adequate for most needs. With one of these, you receive the phone number of the person who is trying to reach you.

2. **An alphanumeric system.** With these, you can receive short text messages as well. Some even have services that allow users to follow sports and business news as well as check e-mail. An advance of these systems notifies the message sender that you received their page—a frequent concern to those trying to reach you.

3. **Two-way pagers.** In addition to receiving short text messages and phone numbers, these units permit users to send back an instant reply over the same airwaves. (Two employees from the same company have been known to pass electronic notes to each other during meetings via these devices.) The recipient can get the response via an Internet e-mail message to his computer or on the screen of his own pager. Some even receive voice mail messages and translate them to the pager screen. Others can be pro-

grammed to keep investors up-to-date on his or her stock portfolio and even execute sales. (Some palm computers have these same capabilities, so if you foresee investing in one of the top-of-the-line electronic calendars, you won't need a two-way pager as well. Refer to Chapter 7 for more information and do a comparison of which product best suits your needs.)

TELEPHONE ANSWERING DEVICES

The more wizardry that's invented, the more complex our choices, and that pertains, too, to what used to be a simple decision: Do I get an answering machine, get voice mail, or use a service?

A few people today—those whose callers need personal contact—still use answering services. Most home offices today, however, are weighing the benefits of answering machines against the benefits of voice mail:

Answering Machines. Some come with a built-in phone; others don't. Some of the benefits of an answering machine are as follows:

—You're in complete control of the system. Once you're home, there's no need to ever call in for messages.

—Lets you screen calls while you work (this may not be important if you have Caller ID, which also accomplishes this purpose silently; you don't need to listen to the message the way you do with an answering machine).

—Gives you a digital readout of the number of messages taken (as does Caller ID).

—Some now come equipped with "mailboxes"—a system that used to be unique to voice mail systems. These systems will answer calls for all of your telephone lines, but callers can leave a message for a specific family member. Therefore, you don't have to scroll through eight calls for your teenager before getting to the messages for your business.

Voice Mail System. You can add a voice mail system to your own home telephone system, or for a monthly fee you can purchase this service from your telephone company. Even with a telephone company system, it can be your voice providing the message, and the system offers the opportunity to establish different mailboxes for various departments of your business or to categorize personal and family calls. One of the biggest advantages of voice mail is that the system takes calls for you even when you're on the phone—you (and not the person with whom you're speaking) will hear a beep and know to pick up messages afterward. Your callers need never get busy signals—a distinct advantage if you're on the phone a lot. Voice mail systems also let you forward messages to other people—an element that may or may not be of benefit to you. One dad who volunteered as a soccer coach when he wasn't running his home-based business used the group message feature to send messages about practices to the team members who also had voice mail.

TECHNOLOGICAL ADVANCES: "WHAT WILL THEY THINK OF NEXT?"

Before leaving the discussion of technological developments, you should know about a new service that is now available to home businesses. Sometimes referred to as a "virtual assistant" and acting like a secretary of sorts, it answers the phone, places calls, takes messages, or offers callers a "search" option ("Should I find him or her for you?"). Then based on preprogrammed information you've entered (ranging from a single number to a series of numbers for the places you'll be that day), the number finds you and relays the message that your client has called, permitting you to get right back to the client if need be.

This "virtual assistant" also keeps track of a calendar and a telephone directory and can look up a number for you, reads e-mail to you over the phone, and you can preprogram it for your special interests so that when you call in for information it will tell you about major news breaks or stock market information you'd like to hear about.

There are also new "unified messaging" services that coordinate messages—faxes, e-mail, voice mail, and pages, and the system lets you respond with a voice mail to a fax, for example. Another advantage to the system is that if your fax or phone line is busy, the calls get forwarded to your unified messaging number, and you can pick it up from there.

It's getting easier and easier to run a home business!

TELEPHONE MANAGEMENT 101: OUTGOING CALLS

The telephone is a tremendous time-saver, but it can also be a major time-waster. Here's what you need to do to keep it from eating up your time:

- Set aside specific time to do your phoning, and don't be distracted.

- Consolidate and prioritize all calls on a "to call" list (your Office Notebook should have a section devoted to the calling you need to do). Note the telephone number next to the name. That way if you have to call back, you won't have to look it up again.

- Business calls should be planned out, just the way you would create an agenda for a meeting. Leave space on your "to call" list so that you can write down the points you need to cover in the discussion. That way you won't forget anything.

- Don't make business calls on your home line. Anyone with Caller ID will then have your home number—a serious inconvenience for those working from home.

- Minimize interruptions on your end. Deactivate call-waiting, and use voice mail or your answering machine to cover other phone lines.

- Get calls off to a good start by asking, "Is this a good time to talk?"

- Establish from the outset how long you can talk.

- When you make the call, get to the point quickly. If you and the other person have time, you can have a chat at the end of the conversation.

- Take notes on business calls. Document the calls in your Office Notebook. More and more people are doing it through contact management programs, software that serves as planner/address book/information manager all in one. The important thing is to have a way to go back and reconstruct what was said when necessary.

- If you're calling from a cell phone on the road and fear that you might drive into valleys where your signal won't carry, then explain this beforehand and tell the person you'll call them back as soon as you can if the two of you get cut off.

- If the person isn't in and you've reached a secretary, ask about the best time to call back. And remember, courtesy is key. The secretary has the power to convey your message quickly and put you through to the boss—or not. Find out his or her name and treat that person with respect.

- If you're still having no luck, try calling before 9:00 A.M. or after 5:00 P.M. when they are more likely to be answering their phones. If you have to leave a message, specify date and times when it's best to call you.

- With the hard-to-reach, make telephone appointments and stick to them.

- E-mail has made the inaccessible accessible. A person can be halfway around the world, but you can zap a message to him and get a reply as soon as he reads it. While the telephone will always be necessary for longer discussions, it's hard to beat the convenience of e-mail for the exchange of short pieces of information.

- If you reach a company voice mail system and don't know the department or person's extension, try hitting zero on your touchtone phone during the message. On many systems, this will bounce your call to the operator who can answer your question.

- Always leave your telephone number. Even people who know you well may not have your telephone number memorized.

- Speak slowly enough that someone would be able to write as they listen to your message. (Remember, too, the audio quality of voice mail isn't always that clear.)

- Leave information that advances the conversation to try to reduce the need to keep trading phone calls.

TELEPHONE MANAGEMENT 101: INCOMING CALLS

- If you receive phone calls from people you don't know, get their name early in the conversation and write it down in your Office Notebook.

- If you have to put a person on hold, do so only briefly.

- If you receive a call from someone who is slow at getting to the point, try saying, "I'm expecting someone in a few minutes . . . " or "I have to leave in just a few minutes . . . How can I help you?"

- If you have a staff person who could handle certain calls, clarify this to your customers: "John always handles returns and is terrific at working out all the details. I'm going to have you speak with him."

TELEPHONE MANAGEMENT, MASTER'S DEGREE: ENDING A CALL

We all have conversations with people with whom it seems impossible to get off the phone. Here are some suggestions for managing those calls:

- While inquiring about someone is thoughtful and courteous, be careful of what you ask—some questions can set off long conversations, and you may not have time for that.

- Be wary of straying from the topic. As soon as someone begins to digress, you may want to start making your excuses such as these "conversation closers."

—I wish I had more time to talk.

—Maybe we can talk about this more next time.

—I've got to leave for an appointment.

—I have someone holding on the other line.

—I have people arriving for a meeting.

—Could we make this short? I have something that must be finished by noon.

—I don't want to hold you up . . . I'll get back to you when I have the rest of the information.

—Just one more thing before we hang up.

—I've taken up enough of your time. I'll let you get back to work.

WHEN YOU'RE NOT THERE: RECORDING YOUR OUTGOING MESSAGE

The image you project in your outgoing message not only conveys an image about your business, but it also will make a difference as to how efficient a message the caller leaves for you. Your children singing holiday songs doesn't promote businesslike efficiency; your voice carefully explaining where you are and when you'll be back does. Here are some tips:

- Keep your outgoing message as short as possible so it doesn't waste a caller's time. If your system will permit them to bypass the message (which when long-winded can get annoying) and go directly to the beep, tell them how to do so.

- Rerecord messages as often as necessary so that callers know what to expect. If you're on the phone, say so. If you're out of town, let them know when you'll be checking in. If your business is such that a caller might want to get in touch with someone else in the meantime, leave that name and number in your message. If you're taking a long weekend, let them know that it will be Tuesday before you get back to them.

- If you do a new recording daily, note the date in your message so that it's clear to callers that it's an up-to-date message.

- Let callers know if they have a limited time in which to leave their message.
- Tell people to leave their number for you; they may think you have their number memorized, but if you don't, you'll have to waste time looking it up.

R ETURNING CALLS

- Check your messages regularly. Use a telephone log or a page in your Office Notebook for keeping track of calls. Don't write your messages on scraps of paper, restaurant napkins, or the backs of envelopes. By writing down the information in a specific spot, you'll be able to find the person's number again or check on other vital information that will be lost if you use scraps of paper.
- A good time to return calls is just before lunch or between 4:30 and 5 P.M. People tend to be in their offices at that time, but they won't be prone to talking for too long because they're trying to leave for lunch or for home.
- If you don't want to speak directly to someone, try calling at lunchtime or late in the evening and leaving the information

on his or her answering machine or voice mail system. Try not to do this if it simply prolongs "telephone tag." However, if you can leave a succinct answer on his or her voice mail that solves that person's problem, thus saving yourself time, then leave a message. (Make sure you say from the outset that there's no need to return the call.)

- Always mention that you're returning the person's phone call. If you get a secretary, you might be put through more rapidly, or if you're speaking directly to the person it will jog his or her memory as to the reason for the call.

TELEPHONE DIRECTORIES

While more and more people are using palmtop computers and digital assistants to keep track of names and phone numbers (refer to Chapter 7 for more information), there are still the old-fashioned ways as well:

- If you use a roll-file for telephone numbers, color code personal and business file cards for easier reference.

- Cross-reference services and/or people you don't know well. Instead of keeping track of Joan Jones, the computer tutor, under "Jones," file her under "Jones" and "Computer tutor" as well.

- Note personal information next to a person's name (spouse's name, special interests, etc.) That way you've got information at your fingertips if you should need it.

- If you still prefer paper over electronics, then remember that a true telephone directory is portable and a roll-file system is not. Invest in a new paper directory—in this day and age, you need a style that has room for name, street address, e-mail address, fax number, cell phone, and beeper number.

TIME-SAVERS

- Keep a clock visible. It will remind you of the time.

- If you're really trying to shorten calls, purchase a kitchen timer to keep on your desk. Estimate how long you want to spend on a certain conversation and set the timer for that amount of time.

- Keep conversations to the point. A preplanned list of questions or topics to discuss will avoid your needing to call back (a big waste of time).

- Your tone will indicate how businesslike and direct you need to be. It's not just what you say but how you say it: Gabby? Direct? Courteous? Efficient? It's your choice.

- When you feel your telephone usage has gotten out of hand, create a log and note your telephone calls for a week: who initiated the call (was it you?), their length, and the nature of the call. This will help you evaluate which calls were necessary and which ones took longer than they should have.

KEEP IT SIMPLE

1. Evaluate what phone services you need, and consider whether you need a cellular phone or beeper (or both), and then shop carefully for them. Keep up with new developments—you may learn of additional developments that will be of great value to you.

2. Screen incoming calls when you're busy, and organize yourself prior to making outgoing calls so that the time you spend on the phone is used efficiently.

3. Learn how to end a call gracefully by using various "closing lines" indicating you've got to get off the phone.

11

FIGHTING INTERRUPTIONS (FROM EVERYONE)

AND DISTRACTIONS (FROM EVERYWHERE)

WHAT'S AHEAD

Create an Interruption-Free Time

Become "Interruption Smart"

Work-at-Home Distractions and How to Minimize Them

Look How Busy I'm Not

Tracking Interruptions

Workers everywhere grapple with what to do about interruptions and distractions—I see it in major corporations, local businesses, and home offices. However, it is the home-based worker who often suffers the most—here's a typical interruption-filled hour for a home-based worker:

Nine A.M., the kids have left for school, and our home-based worker heads directly to her desk intending to get some work done. She turns on the computer to check her e-mail and discovers that something unexpected has occurred with one of her clients, so she takes time to send a lengthy e-mail to the person who has notified her of this (distraction). In the midst of sending the e-mail, her phone rings (interruption). Another client, another problem that requires several minutes. At 9:30 she's off the phone and pulls the file for the project she needs to work on this morning. The doorbell rings (interruption). She runs downstairs to discover the package delivery man has left a package and is already gone. Now did he really have to ring the bell? Before going back upstairs she decides she might as well throw in a load of clothes (self-interruption). By the time she sits down at her desk again and rereads what she was working on, it is 10 A.M.—one full hour gone and the project on which she intended to work is no farther along than it was at 9 A.M.

For most working people, phone calls, deliveries, faxes, and e-mail, not to mention meetings with clients and those ever present "emergencies and urgencies," are an important and normal part of the business day. Though these interruptions and distractions are to be expected, they will also rob you of precious time. In order to work at home effectively, you've got to learn to manage interruptions, ignore certain distractions, and control the urge to self-interrupt. This means:

—Establishing blocks of time when you aren't interrupted so that you can be available to handle day-to-day issues at other times during your work day.

—Trying to anticipate certain types of interruptions in order to better manage and minimize them.

—Maintaining focus! And learning how to quickly get back on track.

CREATE AN INTERRUPTION-FREE TIME

Your first task then is to establish a time when you can work without interruption in order to complete paperwork or projects that require concentration. The amount of time will be different for every person because each one of us needs a varying amount of time for this type of work. (A salesperson needs to spend the bulk of his time on the phone or with people. His or her need for uninterrupted time is different because so much of the work must include interaction with people; a writer needs much more interruption-free time because writing generally requires quiet concentration.) Here are some suggestions:

• Get up before the rest of the world is stirring (or "night" people may prefer to work late into the evening) and accomplish your paperwork then. Even if you live alone, your phone will start ringing by 9 A.M., and others will begin to nip at your time. By working when the rest of the world is snoozing, you'll find the peace you need in order to get your work done.

- Use your voice mail system, answering machine, or Caller ID to screen calls during a certain period of the day.

- Some telephone systems can be programmed so that a particular line won't ring before or after a designated hour—a good solution for turning off a business phone. Or use a machine, or just don't answer the phone after hours.

- Take your work to the library or some other location where you can work uninterrupted.

- Establish a pattern as to when your interruption-free time is. This will be helpful to you in developing this new habit, and if the block of time is during business hours, it will be helpful to clients and family because they'll learn when it is that you're not to be disturbed.

- Write this "appointment" on your calendar, even if it's at 5 A.M. It reminds you of your schedule, and it will be easier to stick to it.

- If family members forget, make a DO NOT DISTURB sign for your door. Close the door and hang the sign when you need uninterrupted time.

- Set a specific goal for each block of time. Your level of efficiency will rise if you know exactly what you want to accomplish.

BECOME "INTERRUPTION SMART"

Sometimes interruptions snowball to create a feeling of "What's the point? I'm not going to get anything done anyway." Here are some steps to take to keep you "on task" so that you do get your work done:

- Group interruptions when you can. You may even want to create an "interruption" day when you plan on getting only low-level work done.

- If something comes up that must be attended to, make a plan for when you'll return to your current project.

- If a person interrupts you, ask: "Could we discuss this later?"

- If interrupted mid-thought, jot down a word or two about what you were thinking so that you will know where you were when you were interrupted.

- Keep returning to what you were doing. Don't let the interruption "win."

- When you've been constantly interrupted while working on something, it's sometimes very difficult to become focused again. Close your door, turn on your answering machine (or let voice mail pick up any calls), and work on the project for fifteen uninterrupted minutes. This should help restore your energy for the project, and any "brainpower" or creativity should return during this time.

WORK-AT-HOME DISTRACTIONS AND HOW TO MINIMIZE THEM

While corporate offices also have their fair share of distractions, home offices specialize in them. You're working at home, a place you love, and there is no end to the number of things that can distract you! All too frequently it seems that other people's priorities are taking away the time you need for your priorities.

Here are some suggestions for getting work done despite this:

- Establish office hours. They can be 5 A.M.–noon or 10 A.M.–3 P.M., whatever suits your schedule, but make it a rule that once you're in your office you'll tend only to business.

- Prepare instructions for household help and set aside a specific time to answer questions so that they needn't interrupt you while you're working.

- The telephone can create nonstop interruptions if you let it:

  —While a five-minute telephone chat with a friend midmorning can provide relief from loneliness, just be certain to limit the number of calls and their duration. Tell everyone you'll call back after office hours.

  —Don't chat or ask an extra question or two of the caller.

  —Use an egg-timer to time your calls so that you'll know when it's time to get back to work.

—Use a kitchen timer to signal to others that you need to get off the phone. While "I've got to go—I have something in the oven" isn't appropriate in this case, just indicate that the bell was set to remind you to do something, and therefore, you've got to go.

- Try to prevent certain distractions and interruptions:

—The meter reader. In some communities the public utility companies still send out "meter readers" who need to be let into the house. However, in more and more communities there are ways the readings can be done from outside so that you no longer have to go and let someone in. Call your utility company and ask.

—The package delivery fellow. Ask if packages can be left on the porch. That way you don't have to run to the door to accept something that could have waited. If package delivery services in your neighborhood require a signature and you're not concerned about theft, ask if you can presign some delivery acceptance slips.

—Repair people. Just because you're at home it doesn't have to mean you're available full-time for workers. Schedule them at your convenience, not theirs.

—A drop-in visitor. Keep it short and just remain standing in the front hall. As soon as you play "hostess" you can kiss the hour good-bye.

—Your family. Explain to them your work hours and tell them you'll see them as soon as you're finished. If you have a child-care worker with your kids while you're working, explain to her that you should only be interrupted in an emergency. Many of them have difficulty saying "no" to a child who "wants to see Mommy"!

—Yourself. Be your own best "professional." Don't accept requests for favors that will steal from your time, and definitely don't add on to your "to do" list by thinking of out-of-house things that need to be done. Self-discipline is the only true solution to dealing with other distractions—whether you're tempted to throw "just one" load of laundry in the wash instead of working, or you decide "one little" trip to the refrigerator won't break your concentration (or hurt your waistline), you've just got to remember that working from home is a privilege and that you'll be unable to continue it if you don't learn how to overcome the temptation to slack off.

• But what about that day when you just want to get back into bed and read? If your schedule will permit it, call in sick to yourself, and declare it a mental health day. Everyone needs a break now and then, and unfortunately home-based workers generally feel guilty about the simplest things—even meeting a friend for lunch. Build in some down time, off time, social time, especially time to spend with the family; it's great for the mind and the spirit.

LOOK HOW BUSY I'M NOT

Self-interruptions are a problem for everyone—I see them everywhere. Unless you happen to be working on something you absolutely love, it can be difficult to concentrate, and as a result, the natural reaction is to self-interrupt: *"I'm sitting down to work on the XYZ account, oh, but I need a drink of water. On the way back from the kitchen, I notice the plant needs watering so I take care of that. A noise outside—I take a look. I sit down at my desk and realize the file I need is across the room. I get up and get it and realize I forgot to make reservations for lunch."* It's endless.

- Develop the skill of concentration by protecting your time so that you have practice at working in a focused manner for 20–60 minute blocks of time. Because of the pace of our life and the number of technological devices that help us communicate with the outside world, we get into a pattern of constantly being interrupted. Therefore, workers barely know how to sit and concentrate at one project for a prolonged period of time. This habit can be broken through practice.

- State what your goal is for the time available to you and make a commitment to work until the goal is achieved.

- When you're ready to work, be certain you have all your tools and materials with you. Jumping up and down for items is a classic (and totally preventable) form of self-interrupting.

- Keep your desk top clear. If your eye is drawn to another project that's laid out, it breaks your concentration. After you finish working on a project, file it.

- Faxes are rarely emergencies. Even when you hear the sound of an incoming fax, wait to pick it up at your next break. Don't give in to your curiosity when you're working on something else.

- Don't misuse your time by initiating any unnecessary phone calls, going online, or taking a break.

- Finish what you start.

- Don't procrastinate. The project isn't going to go away.

TRACKING INTERRUPTIONS

If you still don't feel you have a handle on why you're not in better control of your time, create a log where you can track your interruptions:

Day/time	Interruption	Necessary?	How long?	Solution

- Most people find that their interruptions follow the 80/20 rule. 80 percent of the interruptions come from 20 percent of the people. Once you can identify who is interrupting you (even if the interruptions are self-interruptions) you can begin to work on a "fix."

- If most of your interruptions are occurring at a certain time of day or in a certain block of time (Friday afternoon, for example), consider what should be done about this. Are you experiencing a breakdown with your support system, or is this simply a time that people need to reach you? If your answer is the latter, then rethink your work habits. Maybe this is a time when you should do filing, faxing, answering e-mail, going through papers, or taking out your "on the go" reading file—work that is stress-free so that you're more available and less irritated by those who need you.

- Identify solutions. Can you break the habit of those who keep interrupting you? If the children are constantly peeking in, you may have a problem with your child-care worker. If the telephone never stops, you've got to screen calls using an answering machine or Caller ID. If you have an employee who is constantly asking questions, you need to create a better system. Begin by trying to anticipate when there may be questions and explaining what you need done. Then establish periodic meeting times when you can answer questions and go over other aspects of the work all at one time rather than throughout the day.

KEEP IT SIMPLE

1. Establish a regular interruption-free time for some of your work by getting up early, blocking out calls, or anything else you need to do that lets you work uninterrupted for a time.

2. Control interruptions by grouping those that you can anticipate and minimizing those that occur unexpectedly.

3. Resist the temptation to self-interrupt or to be lured away from your work by the refrigerator, the family, or by a friend on the phone. Self-discipline is the key to getting things done.

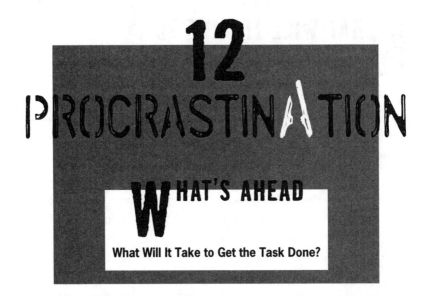

12
PROCRASTINATION

WHAT'S AHEAD

What Will It Take to Get the Task Done?

Procrastination is one of the single biggest enemies of working from home. You can have the perfect office and the latest technology; you can successfully carve out time for your work; you can have a well organized desk; but if you procrastinate your home-based worklife will soon be a bust. Nothing is more exhausting than worrying about what you aren't doing and what isn't getting done.

WHAT WILL IT TAKE TO GET THE TASK DONE?

Even people who master good work habits sometimes procrastinate—a particular task seems overly difficult; there are too many tasks involved in a certain project; or maybe something just seems boring or too time-consuming. Here's what to do:

- Go back through your Master List, and evaluate what you've been avoiding. Ask yourself what it will take to get the task done. Just how uninspired are you? Will a little self-discipline do the trick, or can you hire someone to do it for you? If doing the task really makes no sense right now, then cross it off your list and forget about it. Those items that still need attention should be written together on a new page in your Office Notebook. Draw a box around the remaining tasks and label the box, "Procrastination Items."

- If any of the items catch your interest as you create the list, take care of it right away. You'll gain momentum as you experience the good feeling of accomplishing some of the tasks.

- Make a deal with yourself to tackle at least one of these items each day.

- Always remember to break big or difficult tasks down into manageable parts that can be addressed one by one.

- Set a time limit for working on a project. If you really can't bear the thought of doing something, tell yourself you'll try it for just ten minutes. Then sit down with a clock at your side and see what you can do about the project during that ten-minute period. Maybe you can find some small part of the task that interests you and will help you get going; work until you've had enough. With luck, getting a little bit done will keep you motivated.

- Don't focus on achieving perfection with everything you do. You'll set yourself up for failure or get nothing done at all. Skip the negative thoughts like, "I'll never do it well enough"—this attitude will paralyze you. Instead, just "do it."

- Take advantage of your moods. Repetitive tasks that are time-consuming are perfect for late in the day or when you're watching television.

- Build both long and short breaks into your schedule. One of the major drawbacks to working from home is that your work is always available to you. Procrastination can stem from resentment at how much you have to do and how your work is always *there*. You'll find that if you take sanctioned short breaks during the day as well as time off on weekends and for vacations, all of your work will be easier to do.

- Establish small rewards for tasks that are distasteful. If your basement file cabinet is overflowing with papers you no longer need, but you've procrastinated for months on getting down there to clean it out, set a specific date, maybe some Saturday morning, and then select an appropriate payback for yourself—a new paperback book, lunch with a friend, or an article of clothing you've had your eye on.

- Consider the consequences of continuing to delay. If your continued resistance to working on a client's project is going to mean losing the job or pulling an all-nighter in order to get it done, then the thought of either of those experiences might provide motivation. If the consequences aren't serious and may even be beneficial (there may be a new development or additional information that will be helpful) then you may actually be wise to wait.

- View difficult tasks as an "interesting" challenge. Rather than being overwhelmed by how hard something is going to be, look at it as a way to learn something new.

- Ask yourself what's bothering you about a particular task? Once you understand what's making you procrastinate, it's generally easier to do.

- Keep a list of accomplishments. Reading it over now and then should inspire you.

- Expect interruptions but don't let them pull you permanently from what you're doing or your problem with procrastination will simply become worse. (See Chapter 11 for help in coping with interruptions.)

- Learn to say "no" to things you really don't like to do.
- Remind yourself of how good you'll feel when it's done.

KEEP IT SIMPLE

1. Make a list of the items on which you're procrastinating, and evaluate which really need to be done and which can be crossed off without ever doing them.

2. If you're really having trouble getting something done, then you need help getting started. Break the project down into parts, and work on the project for just ten minutes.

3. Learn to say "no" to things you really don't like to do.

PART FOUR

MANAGING

PAPER

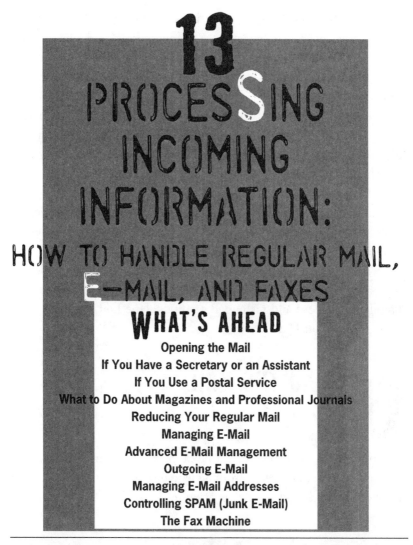

13

PROCESSING INCOMING INFORMATION:

HOW TO HANDLE REGULAR MAIL, E-MAIL, AND FAXES

WHAT'S AHEAD

It seems quite enticing to think back to the leisurely time when businesses used to do a good part of their correspondence by regular mail. Of course, urgent items were sent by messenger or overnight courier, but most letters and packages were deemed suitable to arrive in two to five days.

Today most business correspondence is viewed as more urgent than that—messages zap back and forth by e-mail, longer documents are faxed or sent by overnight courier, and only less pressing items are sent by regular mail.

Unfortunately, the diminishing of urgent first class mail has done nothing to unburden us. We still have just as much information to handle, but now it arrives faster, and people expect it to be processed immediately.

Processing all mail and managing incoming information is vitally important to remaining organized. We'll start by examining how to handle the ancient, old-fashioned, traditional method of communication—the regular U.S. Mail.

OPENING THE MAIL

Toss out your in box! An in box tends to become a permanent parking place for an ever increasing load of mail that's not dealt with until one day when it topples over on to the surface of the desk. As for the out box—since most people in home offices work alone, who are you sending this "out" to?

So what do you need? Here are the items I consider indispensable when opening the mail:

—Letter opener
—Wastebasket
—Pen
—Highlighter/markers
—Stapler
—Sticky-backed notes
—Envelopes for sending quick messages by return mail
—Mailers
—Stamps
—Office notebook
—Tickler file

The following system involves processing as much as you can when it arrives and then putting the rest in file folders until it can be managed.

- Sorting the mail and opening the mail can occur at two different times. No matter who sorts it (you or another family member), sort all of the mail at one time. Business letters should go directly to your office, not the kitchen table, the hall table, or your night table.

- Open the mail in a clutter-free environment so that you can sort the papers without getting them mixed up with other papers.

- Select a specific time for opening the mail. By identifying the mail as a task that can be accomplished at a specific time, you'll increase the likelihood of handling it efficiently.

- All the mail should be opened in one sitting.

- As you sort, here are your options:

  —**Toss?** Use the wastebasket as often as you can. Throw out all extraneous items, envelopes, and enclosures, saving only the part of the letter that you need.

  —**Note and toss**. When you open the letter about the professional meeting you want to attend, write down the date, time, and place in your calendar and toss the letter. If you need specific information such as directions or a description of a guest speaker note it in your calendar or put that part of your letter into your tickler file for the appropriate day or month. It's nothing more than extraneous paper to handle.

  —**Pass on to someone else.** If you have a partner or an employee, or an accounting firm that handles your bills, certain items should be passed on to the other person immediately. (Create a Mail Folder for that purpose.)

  —**Read.** If a piece of mail will take less than five minutes to read or scan, do it now. Longer items should be placed in your "To Read" file.

  —**Act on it.** If you can redirect this instantly by scrawling a note on the bottom of a letter or filling out a form and sending it back, do so. Anything that will take a little more time should be placed in your "To Do" file.

—**To Do items.** Again, if a task can be accomplished in five minutes or less, do it as you're opening the mail. Some projects, however, require more time or more attention than what you can give them when the task at hand is sorting. Put these items in a "To Do" file you go through daily. Also note the related task in your spiral notebook (see Chapter 8), where you keep a running list of "To Do" items.

—**File.** Anything you need for future reference will have to be filed. The agenda for next month's committee meeting should be skimmed and dropped into the "Upcoming Meeting" or Tickler file. (Start an "Upcoming Meeting" file if you're going to have more than a couple of pages to take to the meeting.) That report you requested on a new product should go directly into the appropriate file. Try to file these papers as soon as you take them into your home office.

• If you encounter something where you need more information in order to make a decision, place that item in your Tickler file on the date or in the month at which you want to be reminded of it again. (See Chapter 14.)

IF YOU HAVE A SECRETARY OR AN ASSISTANT

If you have help, then assigning the task of "mail management" makes a lot of sense. Letting someone else tear open a plasticized overnight mail envelope and sift through and set priorities on the mail will save you time.

- Spend time teaching your assistant what it is you want done. It may take up to ten days or more to encounter all the different types of challenges that come in the mail. Work together until you are satisfied.

- Create several file folders. Choose a different color for each folder for added clarity. Your assistant should be trained to sort the mail accordingly:

   —Urgent, for anything that needs to be looked at immediately

   —To Answer or To Do

   —To Approve and/or To Sign

   —To Pay. Establish a system for pulling out bills; then establish a regular day for paying them so that everything gets paid on time.

   —To Read

   —To File (but for you to check first)

—Undecided. This lets you skim through and take action on papers that your assistant is unsure about.

- If you get a lot of mail in the "Urgent" and "To Do" category, ask your assistant to create a list of what's inside, highlighting any due dates so that in a glance you can prioritize.

- Establish a system for returning the completed folders to the assistant with your instructions attached.

IF YOU USE A POSTAL SERVICE

Some home business owners prefer using the post office box or one of the storefront mailbox services that have opened in most communities. The inconvenience of leaving home to pick up your mail is outweighed by the need for privacy. Then no one has your home address, and your business mail is kept separate from your personal mail.

While post office boxes are easily available to most people, the private postal services offer a couple of advantages. You usually use their street address followed by a suite number as your address. This gives you the hallmark of being an established business instead of a recent business that has yet to set down roots. Another convenience offered by these services is that they will receive and sign for all types of packages for you, regardless of the carrier.

A special tip: If you pick up your mail at an outside location, sort through it before getting into your car. The more you can throw away before coming home, the less time you'll have to spend processing the mail.

WHAT TO DO ABOUT MAGAZINES AND PROFESSIONAL JOURNALS

I've been in countless homes and offices where stacks and stacks of reading material accumulate. With each day's mail delivery, more reading material arrives and none seems to ever leave. If this is happening in your home office, here's what you need to do:

- Keep your personal magazines in a separate part of the house, not in your home office. This just adds unnecessary clutter to your work space.

- Consider the magazines to which you've subscribed and evaluate whether or not you still want to receive them. Often people renew out of habit, which just keeps more paper coming into your home office.

- Now that so much can be retrieved over the Internet, saving magazines for long periods of time is rarely necessary. If, however, you do have a particular publication you like to save, then keep only six months' worth. Donate or recycle magazines you don't need anymore.

- Set aside a time once a week to read through this material. This is vital to staying organized. If you don't devote time to getting through what comes in, you'll lose the battle of "paper onslaught."

- Create an "On the Go" reading file. If you can't find time to get your reading done, place unread materials in this file. Take it with you when you know you'll have waiting time.

REDUCING YOUR REGULAR MAIL

- Cancel subscriptions to everything you aren't interested in or don't need anymore.

- Withdraw your membership from organizations that are no longer of current value.

- Create a form letter to send to companies asking that they remove your name from their mailing list.

- Write to the Mail Preference Service, Direct Marketing Association, P.O. Box 9008, Farmingdale, NY 11735-9008. Provide them with all variations of your name and ask to be removed from mailing lists. Your name will be put on a Mail Preference Service list that is circulated among national direct-mail companies who are supposed to delete your name from their lists. While it won't end all your unsolicited mail, it will help.

MANAGING E-MAIL

E-mail is a tremendous time-saver: One e-mail message can replace a ten-minute phone call; the frustration over misplaced messages; and the time spent explaining yourself to a secretary or assistant. E-mail also solves the problem of telephone tag. You no longer need to worry about catching someone when they're in—when they're in, they'll get your message.

However, e-mail, too, can become overwhelming if not managed properly. It's common today for businesspeople to log on in the morning and find 60–80 messages. Here's what you need to do to make sure you handle it efficiently:

- Try to answer your e-mail messages daily, even when you're traveling. Checking in regularly will keep you in touch, and it will prevent a major backlog waiting for you when you come back.

- Just as you do with regular mail, establish specific times for checking and answering your e-mail. Checking e-mail is a lot more fun than working, and many home-based workers find that it can eat up a major portion of the work day.

- Scan the incoming messages. Read and answer them in order of importance. Delete all jokes, "free offers," and miscellaneous mail you don't need. If you run out of time, save the other messages to answer at a later date.

- When you receive something important by e-mail, print out a copy and file it in the appropriate file so that you can retrieve it when you need it.

- Some correspondence shouldn't be answered immediately. It's okay to take a more leisurely approach, even with e-mail. The cousin that e-mails you with news now and then should be answered in a few days—zapping a reply back instantly puts an urgency on the correspondence that isn't justified. Though difficult to remember, some messages require no reply at all.

- If you receive a lot of e-mail, establish different e-mail addresses for different purposes. One address might be reserved for your business; others might be for personal matters or volunteer work.

ADVANCED E-MAIL MANAGEMENT

- Establish filters that sort your e-mail into separate folders. A filter can be established to look for a certain string of words, enabling you to sort and group e-mail from a particular client or concerning a certain product, for example.

- Filters can also be set to respond automatically. An e-mail with product information could go out to messages you get concerning one of your products, or you can program your computer to send out "I'm on vacation" notices to e-mail that comes in while you're away. (Even if you answer from the road, your correspondents will be made aware that they may not hear from you immediately.)

OUTGOING E-MAIL

- Concise e-mail messages generally get concise answers in return, so don't be wordy. Your most important information should be in the first paragraph with the less important below. Most e-mail messages should be only three paragraphs or less.

- Use the attachment feature to sending longer documents or letters.

- Try to limit your message to one topic; it makes it easier for the recipient to file it appropriately.

- Use the subject line to convey some of your message. Rather than putting "meeting" in the subject line, note instead: "need your confirmation by Tuesday."

- Don't use the "urgent" message notation unless it really is.

- While most people view e-mail as less formal than a real letter, don't be sloppy. Take a minute to reread what you've written to make certain your meaning is clear.

- Don't send out needless e-mail messages or copies to people who don't really need to receive your message. You want recipients to value what you send.

MANAGING E-MAIL ADDRESSES

- While you'll want e-mail addresses in your online address book to simplify sending, also make note of them in your regular address book. That provides you with e-mail addresses wherever you are, and if you ever switch mail management services, it provides you with the needed information for making the change.

CONTROLLING SPAM (JUNK E-MAIL)

- Don't register at every web site you visit, and be cautious about to whom you give your e-mail address.

- Filtering out mail from certain addresses doesn't work because spammers move around. Junk e-mail often comes from legitimate addresses. By using a filter that puts into a Trash folder all e-mail that has certain word strings, you can then scan only the headers. If that doesn't reduce your e-mail, you'll need to have it scan the full text of the message. Start out with word strings like "money-making opportunity," "make money," "90 days," "!!!," "$$" (double dollar signs—what client would send you an e-mail with that in it?), and "dear friend." As you receive more and more junk mail, you'll have new word strings you'll want to add.

- Check your Trash folder periodically (when you're on hold on the phone) to make sure the filter isn't filtering out messages you need.

- If you ask to be removed from a junk mail list, and they don't remove you, complain to your service provider. They don't want to be delivering bulk e-mail any more than you want to be receiving it.

- There are as yet no federal statutes specifically covering bulk e-mail, however, any mail that is fraudulent or obscene is covered under existing laws, and you can complain directly to the government at uce@ftc.gov.

THE FAX MACHINE

E-mail is quickly replacing the fax machine as the tool of choice for back-and-forth messages; however, longer documents or documents with handwritten annotations are still going to be sent by fax.

And while the hum of the fax machine turning on tends to encourage many home-based workers to get up from their desks to see what's coming in, you need to resist this urge. Faxes, like all other types of incoming information, should be managed on your terms, not on the sender's terms. While most of the principles presented earlier apply, also keep in mind:

- If you have a programmable fax, enter in your most frequently used telephone numbers so you can fax through by pushing only one or two buttons.

- Purchase a small telephone directory to keep by the telephone with all the other fax numbers you use. It saves steps when sending a fax.

- Write the telephone number to which you're faxing on the back of the document. That way if it needs to be re-sent you don't need to look up the number again—you've got it right there.

- If you're going to be away for a few days, be certain to check your paper supply.

KEEP IT SIMPLE

1. Establish a specific time for going through the mail, and try to process as much of it as you can in that one sitting.

---

2. Do the same with e-mail; check it at preplanned times, and handle incoming messages in order of priority, based on who it's from or what the headline is. (People waste an enormous amount of time by checking their e-mail too frequently.)

3. Try to reduce the amount of mail and e-mail you receive. Cancel subscriptions to magazines you don't have time to read; ask to be removed from catalog and direct mail mailing lists; and on the Internet, try to stay off the joke and other e-mail lists.

14

YOUR NEW FILING SYSTEM:
WHEN "CLIP AND SAVE" LINKS WITH THE INTERNET

What's Ahead

Selecting the Right File Cabinets
Getting Equipped
Getting Started
Filing Tips
Creating Action or Tickler Files

I need not tell you that we sit squarely in the eye of a hurricane, an information hurricane that is. Huge quantities of paper enter most households in the form of newspapers, daily mail, catalogs, advertiser handouts, and school notices by the truckload. Then there's the fax machine and the computer, both of which are capable of generating still more quantities of paper, all of which needs to be processed. Twenty-five years ago no one could have imagined the changes we would see in what people have to cope with.

Up until recently, when it came to filing, my basic principles remained the same: *Create a system and keep up with it.* Today my advice continues, but with a twist: You still need to create a file system, and you still need to keep up with it, but today technology is going to let you toss more than ever before. Because new and better information is constantly accessible to us via the Internet, there's less need to maintain all types of files. There's no sense in saving an article regarding a copier you might buy in a year or two. When the time comes, you can stop by your local library or log on from home and get up-to-the-minute information that will be more helpful than anything you could clip-and-save today.

Here are some new guidelines on what you need to save:

1. **File the personal.** Papers that are unique to you should be retained in the old-fashioned way.

2. **File the irreplaceable.** A letter of agreement, a written estimate regarding a new project (i.e. a new press kit), and the testimonial letter written by a past client all belong in files.

3. **File the current.** While you're working on a brochure for a client, you'll want to maintain copies of correspondence, notes, previous brochures, as well as the design plans, the "hard copy," and the photographs for the brochure that's underway.

4. **File the legal.** Birth certificates, deeds, and contracts need to be stored.

5. **Have an "emergency" file.** If your computer were to go down, what information would you need to have on paper (emergency contact information, medical data, etc.)? This material belongs in a file, too.

6. **Toss (or scan into your computer) almost everything else.** If you're considering saving an article about a company you might invest in "when you have the money," don't. Make note of the company name in your Office Notebook (described in Chapter 8) and check online for information later on. Scan into your computer items like packing lists, "what to do when you're away" lists for sitters, after-school schedules, and all types of instructions. You can update them and then simply print out a clean copy.

Even lengthy information produced by other companies can be worth scanning in if it pertains to a current project. Anyone who has ever pressed "search" or "find" for a certain word or phrase in a computer document knows that these commands will locate relevant information in a split second—reading through an article or brochure can take what seems like forever.

If you haven't already programmed your computer to back up regularly, you need to do so now. There's nothing wrong with being "dependent" on your computer so long as you back up regularly.

As you read through this chapter, remember that my new mantra is "toss whenever possible." Nonetheless, everyone still needs a file system, so here's what you need to do in order to make it work with today's technology.

SELECTING THE RIGHT FILE CABINETS

When you designed a floor layout for your home office in Chapter 5, you did so with a certain style of file cabinet in mind. Whether you chose vertical units (the file drawers pull out from the front; maximum storage for the least amount of space) or lateral file cabinets (the drawers pull out to the side; convenient desk-side storage), you may still be deciding between two-drawer or four-drawer units and legal or letter-size units within the drawers.

- A four-drawer unit, of course, offers the most storage; however, a two-drawer unit offers the benefit of doubling as a counter if you need it. By placing a two-drawer lateral file behind your desk, you not only have easy access to files, but you have the benefit of a credenza-like piece of furniture with space for "action" files, letters to mail, and a few reference books as well. If you need the file storage, the four-drawer models are your best investment.

- To select the size of files, consider whether you primarily file legal or letter-size documents.

- If your files need to be secure, be certain that your units have locks on them.

- Plan to create a suspension filing system ("hanging" files that hold regular file folders). Filing and retrieval are simplified, and the suspension files prevent the "domino effect" within a drawer.

- Decide on a color-coding system: green for financial; blue for clients; red for family medical records, etc. Count on using different colored labels for different subjects. Some people like to use folders of different colors as well. Color-coding your files can help guard against misfiling. If you start to put a green file (financial) in with the blue files (clients), you'll quickly catch your mistake. Making this decision now is important so that you can purchase the needed supplies.

GETTING EQUIPPED

Even if you have existing files, it's a good idea to start with all new supplies. There's something inspiring about opening a drawer of brand-new files with newly printed labels. The very sight makes you want to keep the files straightened out. Here's what you need:

- **Suspension folders to hold files.** The style with the square-cut bottom offer added accessibility because the files aren't squeezed into a V-shape at the bottom.
- **New file folders.** Choose one-third or one-fifth cut folders. Buy files in various colors if you're color-coding your entire system.
- **File labels in the needed colors.**
- **Plastic tabs and insert labels** for the suspension files so that you can label files by category as well as by file.

GETTING STARTED—WHAT EVERYONE HATES TO DO

If you're reorganizing an old system with lots of files and papers that will need to be sorted, schedule several sessions in which to work. While one-hour sessions are ideal, this is also a perfect task for when you have as little as five to fifteen minutes. The job will seem less burdensome if you realize you can accomplish part of it by using small chunks of time.

Step One: Sort through old files.

—As you consider each file, ask yourself:

1. Is this topic/file still relevant to me?
2. Is there any other reason why I need to keep it? (You may not consider last year's tax records "relevant," but of course, you have to keep the file for legal reasons.)

3. If I ever want this information is there a way I can find it elsewhere in just a few minutes? Toss anything you can retrieve on the Internet.

4. Sort through the papers within files you're keeping, eliminating what you can.

5. Next consider where to store it by asking: If I am keeping this file, should it go with my active files in my home office, or should it be placed in "dead storage" elsewhere in the house? Old tax documents don't need to be accessible unless you are contacted by the IRS. Store them in an out-of-the-way location.

Step Two: Sort through unfiled papers.

As you go through these piles, keep asking:

—Is this information unique to me (about my client, my finances, my legal situation, my family)? For easy retrieval, think carefully about how you categorize each paper. Personal papers including medical information should be filed under the name of the family member. Client papers should be stored under the name of the client, but if you've done many projects for a particular client, then divide the file into several categories, creating a "Smith Brochure" file as well as a file for the "Smith Advertising Campaign."

—Set aside papers you can't categorize. Later on, a logical placement will occur to you.

Step Three: Labeling

Write or type labels clearly. Because the precision letters of a typewriter look alike from a distance, handwritten labels may actually be the easiest to identify. There are also "labeling" machines that lessen the work and look great.

Step Four: Group Files Logically or Alphabetically

—Files should be grouped by category and then alphabetized. For example, in a law office all client folders would be grouped and then the folders themselves would be alphabetized. Family files should be together as should all financial files, etc.

—Select where you'll store each category depending on how accessible the files need to be. The file drawers nearest your desk should hold those files you use most frequently. Those you use less regularly can be farther away.

ILING TIPS

• Every time you start a new project, create a new folder for it. This is an improvement over stacking things "for now."

• Every paper that is to be filed should have the date and the source noted at the top. Highlight certain sections of an article or write notes at the top of the letter so you know exactly why you saved it.

- If there's a date at which you'll no longer need the paper, write a "Destroy after _____" note on the paper.

- File regularly. Have a "To File" tray, and make it a practice to file each night before you close up.

- Everyone's filing system is unique because you need to file papers in files that set off *your* mental triggers. When deciding where to file a paper ask yourself, "How do I plan to use this?" not "Where should this go?" For example, a book review of a book you will need for reference should go in the file for the project to which it relates, not in the "Books I'd Like to Read" file.

- Unfold all papers that will be filed.

- Staple together documents that are more than one page. Paper clips tend to stick to other things.

- If you have to remove a paper for any length of time, create a flag for the file that notes where the paper is temporarily.

- Turn over a new leaf. Learn to purge your files whenever you get one out. Any file more than two inches thick should be sorted through. If you can't toss much of it, break it down into smaller categories. On the outside of the folder note the date on which you last sifted through it. That way you'll be certain that your files get cleaned out regularly.

- If you're no longer using certain files regularly, consider whether you can toss out the information. If not, move the file to a less accessible location.

- For documents that mustn't be lost or replaced, use file folders with two-punch fasteners at the top. Place the most recent paper on top. These folders take extra time to use, but they are a good system for papers you must hold on to.

- Leave 3–4 inches of extra space in file drawers to avoid over-stuffing.

- If for any reason you need to save back issues of magazines, store them in magazine file boxes available at office supply stores. Label the boxes as to magazine and date, and file them chronologically. Then purchase a looseleaf binder and some sheet protector pages. Photocopy the table of contents from each magazine and put it in a binder so that a quick glance of the binder will provide you with the contents of each magazine.

- If an employee or other family member uses your files, explain the system to them and tell them to leave a note for you if they have a particular file out for any reason.

CREATING ACTION OR TICKLER FILES

While handheld computers, regular computer programs, and personal digital assistants all have terrific "reminder" methods that you're welcome to use, there's still no substitute for a paper-based reminder system. Even with your hand-held computer system reminding you to "buy Mom's birthday present today," the hand-held computer lacks a way to store the ad for the "perfect present" you found. Paper-based files can hold lengthy directions for driving to a party, the camp application you want to fill out "as soon as the holidays are over," and the clipping about the store you're going to track down next week. Here's how to create a terrific Action/Tickler File system for pending items:

- What you need: 43 folders, one for each month of the year to hold long-range items, and 31 for each day of the month, for short-range details. Select one color for the monthly folders and another color for the daily files. Label 12 by month, and number the rest, 1-31.

- What you do: If it's January 5, and you want to date file a letter that requires follow up on January 22, place the letter in the folder marked "22." Or if you plan to follow up in February, then the letter should be placed in the "February" file. On February 1, pull the "February" folder and sort through it. Place all those papers into files that correspond with the appropriate dates.

These files provide a vital system for keeping stacks off your desk.

K EEP IT SIMPLE

1. Purchase real file cabinets if you don't already have them, and take the time to create a filing system that fits your needs.
2. Keep up with your filing, tossing as much as you can.
3. Action or Tickler files are the best way to keep track of ongoing projects and items on which you need to follow up.

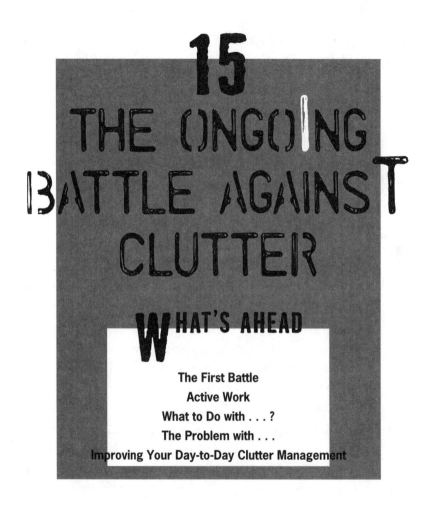

15

THE ONGOING BATTLE AGAINST CLUTTER

WHAT'S AHEAD

The First Battle
Active Work
What to Do with . . . ?
The Problem with . . .
Improving Your Day-to-Day Clutter Management

When I visit homes and offices, I see clutter at its "best"—desks so full of paper that the "owner" starts stacking on the floor, on the chairs, and even on a treadmill. I've been to places where you literally couldn't sit down without moving something first.

While this is "clutter" in the extreme, from a time management standpoint, even a stack or two can start to multiply. If you intend to create a home office where you can function optimally, then you need to wage a constant war against clutter.

THE FIRST BATTLE

Unless you're setting up a brand new office, then chances are you have a clutter problem right now. Here's what to do about it:

- Set aside a block of time, at least an hour, for your first work session. (If you keep procrastinating, make yourself work on the backlog for just ten minutes; as you watch papers disappear, you'll almost certainly find it so gratifying that you'll stay at it for the full hour.)

- Start with the papers on the top of the pile, and process them accordingly. (Note that the process here is almost the same as when you're processing the mail, and had you processed it as it arrived, you wouldn't have to be reading this chapter.)

  —**Toss.** Once you take a second look at some of these papers, you'll be surprised at how much you've saved that really can and should be tossed, particularly as you go through the pile.

—**Act on**. Answer invitations, jot a note of congratulations to the person for the article you just read; set up medical appointments, do whatever it is you meant to do when you placed the paper in the pile in the first place. (In the future use this as a rule of thumb: if a task will take less than two minutes to complete, do it right away. Waiting to do it just wastes more time.)

—**File.** If you don't have an existing file for a particular topic, create one and put it away.

• As your first session ends, you may be able to organize some of the papers into groups: "letters to answer" or "filing" for example. Place them in labeled file folders. At your next work session you'll have a better idea of what you have.

• On your calendar write down an appointment for another work session, and keep at it until the clutter is gone.

• As you progress you may find you have a tremendous stack that needs to be read. Schedule some separate sessions just to catch up with your reading.

• Your goal is a clear desk with only your calendar or printout of your calendar, your office notebook, and your "to do" list on it. You'll be surprised at how much better you feel when you sit down to work each morning and have nothing on your desk. It gives you the freedom to choose whatever file and project you need to begin a new day.

ACTIVE WORK

- I like to have four "active" file folders in my closest file drawer or on a credenza or nearby shelf. These files help reduce most types of office clutter:

    —**"To Copy" folder** for all the items that come across your desk for which you need to make a photocopy.

    —**"To File" folder** for all the papers you need to save, and then make sure you keep up with your filing. You might consider scanning some of the papers into your computer instead of filing them (as was suggested in the filing chapter). More and more people are finding that this further reduces the paper they have around their office.

    —**"To Enter/Computer" folder** for all the information you need to input into your computer—the addresses of new contacts, the record of your most recent expenses, and the websites you want to check out.

    —**"To Read" folder** for all the articles and business reading you don't want to take time to read while you're at your desk but that you do want to read promptly. Set this up as your "On the Go" file. Take it with you anytime you think you might have a few moments to read.

- Start files for all new projects. Too many times people start a "pile" rather than a file when they are undertaking something new. The moment you know you're going to be working on a project (even one that is due in 24 hours), create the file.

- One reason people tell me they "pile" is because it reminds them of what they're working on. Instead, keep a running list of your ongoing projects in your Office Notebook and refer to it regularly.

- Ongoing projects should be kept in the file drawer nearest you for handy reference.

WHAT TO DO WITH . . . ?

- **Reminder papers (travel directions, agendas, etc.).** Put these in the file that pertains to the upcoming meeting or event or in your Tickler File for that date.

- **Business cards.** If you expect to contact the person regularly from now on, enter all the information from the business card in your address book, Rolodex, or computer program and throw the card out. If you simply want to hang on to the card "just in case," file it in a business-card holder, available from office supply stores.

- **Reference books.** Be sure your office has a shelf near your desk where you can put reference books and telephone directories.

THE PROBLEM WITH . . .

- **Stacking bins.** While the theory of having a place to put something "for now" is tempting, I find that the papers placed in stacking bins stay "forever." Leave them out of your home office.

- **Bulletin boards.** If you have a bulletin board, take a look at it now. How many items on it have yellowed with age? When was the last time you put something new up on it? My point is made. The problem with bulletin boards is that after the first flurry of posting items, no one ever takes anything down. Skip the bulletin board altogether.

- **Personal mementos.** While a photo or two can add a nice touch to an office or desk, be careful what you bring into your office. Too many mementos simply become clutter. If you do enjoy having a few personal items in your office, be sure to reevaluate them now and then. You'll actually enjoy them more if you change them and move them around.

IMPROVING YOUR DAY-TO-DAY CLUTTER MANAGEMENT

- Establish time daily for doing paperwork.

- Don't let papers pile up. Be vigilant about getting through the mail and dealing with papers people fax or give to you so that you never again have a miscellaneous pile of papers cluttering your office.

- Clear off your desk at the end of each day. Refile what you took out. Make notes about what you intend to do next for any ongoing project, and put it away.

You'll be surprised how your productivity will improve when you're able to start work the next day with a clean desk.

KEEP IT SIMPLE

1. Schedule time to clear out past clutter. Go through each paper and toss, act on it, or file it. You'll find that much of what is in this pile can go in the trash, so the work will go faster than you might expect.

2. Keep four "active" file folders near your desk: for papers to be copied, papers to be filed, papers with information that needs to

be entered into your computer, and a final file for reading material. Then schedule time regularly for working your way through the tasks in these files.

3. Start a file for all new projects, and note the task in your Office Notebook. That way you can put the papers away but still be reminded of the work you need to do.

PART FIVE

WORKING

WITH

OTHERS

16

MEETINGS AT HOME

AND OUTSIDE THE HOME

WHAT'S AHEAD

To Meet or Not to Meet and if so, How?
In Person? If so, Where?
Setting Date and Time
Setting an Agenda
Keeping Track of Papers
If You're in Charge of the Meeting
Attending a Meeting
Ending the One-on-One
Meeting by Telephone Conference Call
Video Conferencing
Meeting on the Net

For the home-based worker, meetings no longer mean strolling down the hall to your company's conference room or visiting the boss's office for a departmental powwow. Now meetings must be evaluated in a whole new manner: Because of the travel time involved, some meetings will be better off scheduled as a telephone conference call or as a virtual Internet meeting. Others will be well worth making the time to attend, simply because the opportunity to be seen will be vital to business success.

Here are the types of meetings that can be scheduled along with ways to use them effectively:

TO MEET OR NOT TO MEET, AND IF SO HOW?

Meetings today are being conducted in many ways, and some of the new formats are particularly helpful for home-based businesses. When you decide a meeting is necessary, there are several different ways it can be held:

—Face-to-face meetings
—Meetings by conference call
—Meetings by Internet
—Internet video
—Video conferencing

IN PERSON? IF SO, WHERE?

- First, determine that an in-person meeting is necessary. While networking often makes the time investment of attending a meeting worth your while, some issues can be quickly settled by phone or by Web, and to travel any distance would be a waste of your time.

- Clarify your goals for the meeting (landing an assignment, being brought up-to-date on a certain project, ironing out details of a plan) so that you'll be able to stay on target.

- Where to meet? If you're the one scheduling the meeting, then you may have some control over where it will be held. Most home offices aren't conveniently located for a gathering of people, and it can be difficult to create the right atmosphere at home. Once the group settles comfortably in your living room or has a cup of coffee at your dining room table, extra time will be wasted, and it may be difficult to get everyone out at the end of the meeting. For that reason, it is preferable to be on someone else's turf. Consider:

  —A meeting at the client's office is generally well received by the client.

  —Space at company headquarters is usually an option for telecommuters.

—Hotel lobbies can be convenient. Many have coffee bars nearby, and a hotel lobby can be a little more peaceful than a restaurant where a waiter may be checking on you throughout.

SETTING DATE AND TIME

- The date and time at which you schedule the meeting can affect attendance. Avoid Monday mornings and Friday afternoons. Most people need Monday morning to get settled with their work, and by Friday afternoon you can never tell who will be drifting away for the weekend.

- To be efficient, get-togethers scheduled an hour or so before lunch or quitting time generally assures that people will work through the agenda efficiently in order to get out of the meeting on time. A mid-morning meeting also offers a home-based worker the advantage of being able to maximize the networking opportunities by staying to have lunch with one of the people from the company.

- Telecommuters may be able to schedule meetings using a company networking software program. The computer program can determine a mutually convenient time for all who should attend and send each an advisory of the meeting; it also requests confirmation of the intent to attend.

SETTING AN AGENDA

For any meeting you schedule, prepare an agenda:

- Specify when the meeting will start and end. (Stipulating an end time is as important as giving a starting time; people will remain focused if they know they need to do so for only a limited period.)

- Outline what is to be resolved, addressing the most important issues first.

- Lengthy agendas should be sent out in advance.

KEEPING TRACK OF PAPERS

Stacking papers for meetings seems to be one of the more popular ways people hold on to the items they need for meetings. Instead:

- Write down anything you need to bring with you in your calendar by the notation about the meeting.

- Start a file for the meeting, and as papers are acquired, put everything in the file.

- If you'll be making any sort of presentation, keep your notes for it clipped together within the file folder. Even when speaking for only a couple of minutes, take time to think through and write down what you plan to say.

IF YOU'RE IN CHARGE OF THE MEETING

- Start on time. It's a powerful organizational message. If you're in an office or conference room, close the door at the beginning of the meeting even if everyone has not arrived. Those who are there will appreciate not having to wait, and this will signal to latecomers that it's important to be prompt.

- Set the tone by stating the purpose of the meeting and indicating that you plan to stay on schedule.

- If participants don't know each other, they should be given the opportunity to introduce themselves and explain their involvement.

- Ask someone to take notes; another can hand out literature to anyone who arrives late.

- Keep it interesting by drawing out others at the meeting and using visual aids such as a Power Point presentation, flip charts, or an overhead projector to present key points. Product demonstrations, when appropriate, are also helpful.

- If a participant is inappropriately dominating the meeting, try saying: "We have a limited amount of time today. Could I ask that only those who haven't spoken yet address the group now?"

- Keep everyone on topic.
- Try to reach a decision on each agenda item.
- At the end of the meeting, summarize what has been decided, and follow up with a written summation that is e-mailed or faxed to all participants.
- End the meeting promptly, stipulating the next meeting date if necessary.

A TTENDING A MEETING

If you're invited to attend a meeting at your company headquarters or at a client's office, your first task is to decide whether or not to go. Though "being seen" is often valuable for home-based workers, it does take you away from your desk for an extended period of time, so there are times when you'll need to decline.

- Once you've agreed to attend a meeting, call the day before to confirm that the meeting is still being held. (Making a trip for nothing is something you can't afford to do.) If the other party has promised to prepare materials necessary for the meeting, also confirm that the materials are ready.
- If the meeting is expected to be lengthy and you're unable to

attend it in its entirety, check to see if you can participate for just part of the meeting.

- If you're at a meeting where issues are not being resolved, don't hesitate to speak up and ask what the group plans to do. Otherwise, you're guaranteed another meeting will have to be called.

- Offer to take notes at meetings that tend to be disorganized. By participating actively you can ask questions and keep things moving along without seeming to take over.

- Always bring something with you to work on in case you're kept waiting for a meeting to begin.

ENDING THE ONE-ON-ONE

If you're trapped with someone in your home office, be assertive and try these methods:

—"I'm sorry to have to rush you, but I have to be across town in fifteen minutes."

—"Do you need directions for leaving the area?"

Stand, get their coat, and start walking toward the door.

MEETING BY TELEPHONE CONFERENCE CALL

The advantage of a conference call is convenience. Attendees stay in their own environment while still being able to participate in a collaborative meeting. However, because participants can't see one another, conducting a good conference call takes thought and some practice:

- Conference calls among more than three people need to be set up by an operator, and it can take a few minutes to do this. Call the operator about five minutes before the meeting is to begin, and remind the operator to tell people they'll be on hold for a few minutes before the meeting is underway. Traditionally, lower-level people are called first; higher-ranking people are called last so that they are on hold for the least amount of time.

- In advance fax the agenda as well as any backup material participants should have. Financial reports or spreadsheets should also be faxed ahead of time. It can be very difficult to comprehend "numbers" discussions without anything in writing.

- Try to avoid needing a speakerphone for a conference call. (Speakerphones are used when more than one person in an office is participating.) Unfortunately, a speakerphone can diminish the quality of the call because some people may not be able to hear everything that is being said.

- Ask that everyone turn off call-waiting and all other types of interruptions that could disrupt the call.

- Before speaking, people should state their names, and mention if they are addressing their comments to a particular person. Without body language, it can be very confusing, and it can be hard to keep the voices straight.

- Comments should be kept brief, and participants should be reminded to stay on topic.

- Call upon people who aren't speaking. They may find it awkward to jump into the conversation. Let them know their opinions are valuable.

- At the end, review what has been accomplished. E-mail or fax specific "to do" lists to people afterward.

VIDEO CONFERENCING

Video conferencing is a little less convenient than a telephone conference call as you will probably have to travel to an office that has video conferencing capabilities. (Major companies often have these facilities, but if you're setting it up yourself, facilities can be rented.)

- Be certain someone at each location understands how to work all the equipment and have them do a test run.

- People should plan to arrive five minutes before the meeting is to begin.

- Provide tent cards even for a small group, unless everyone already knows everyone else. People can be disoriented by the video camera and providing "name cards" will help.

- If handouts are to be distributed, make certain all locations have them. These papers should be sent in advance to the room where the conference is to take place so that no one has to leave the room in order to get them.

- Time may be limited, so as always, it's important to stay to the point. Don't permit side conversations. They usually aren't picked up by the camera, and it will prove distracting to those who are trying to focus on the meeting.

- Address the camera only when you're speaking to someone at a different location. When you're speaking to someone else in the room, talk directly to that person. (A common mistake people make is directing all their comments to the camera.)

MEETING ON THE NET

There are three types of meetings that can take place online.

1. **Electronic conferencing.** Private chat rooms can be established through company e-mail systems, through the Internet, or with an online service so that specific groups of people can converse on-line. With this electronic room, each member expresses him- or herself through typed text, and sessions can be saved, printed, and reviewed. Advanced systems feature a still photograph of each participant when their name appears. This type of meeting is most like a telephone conference call except instead of speaking to the other people, you're all communicating via keyboards.

2. **Desktop video conferencing.** Desktop video conferencing requires additional hardware and software for your PC, but it still offers a relatively inexpensive form of "meeting." Once you have the equipment installed, you can video conference all day through the Internet for only the Internet connection costs. If you're telecommuting and your boss would like you to check in regularly, the small investment your company makes in the equipment will be earned back in the long run.

3. **Establishing a collaborative work site.** Various Internet sites allow anyone to set up an easy-to-use collaborative work space on the Web. Each person to whom you want to give access is given a

password, and they come and go as needed. Charges are generally per month, and the money spent would be no greater than what it might cost for overnight mail packages and long distance calling. Team members can post a calendar of deadlines, action items for individuals, documents to be reviewed, and any other relevant information.

KEEP IT SIMPLE

1. Make certain that any in-person meeting you schedule is necessary and cannot be accomplished by a telephone call, a "chat room" meeting, or a video conference.

2. Organize in advance for any type of meeting. Prepare an agenda, and create a file where you can put any papers you will need for the meeting.

3. Start your meetings on time; keep people focused; and have someone take notes. Follow up afterwards by fax or by e-mail with any tasks that need to be done.

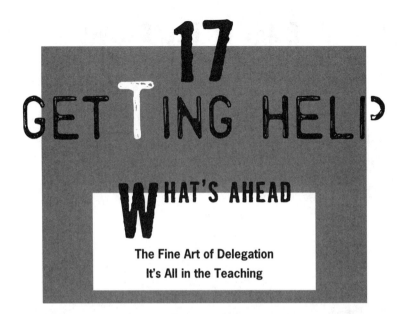

17
GETTING HELP

WHAT'S AHEAD

The Fine Art of Delegation
It's All in the Teaching

One of the best known rules of time management is to delegate—get someone else to help out with the work you don't like to do, don't have time to do, or tasks that can be done less expensively by someone else. But what do you do when you look around your office and discover that you are the secretary, the receptionist, the clerk, the accountant, the marketing genius, the company president, and the custodian all rolled into one?

Delegating certainly isn't as easy as when you are in a corporate office with a well-orchestrated hierarchy, but where there's necessity there's bound to be invention.

THE FINE ART OF DELEGATION

A big step for most home-based workers is realizing they really don't have to do everything. Take a look at your current Master List, and put a dot next to any items that could be done just as well by someone else. Among the day-to-day items that could be delegated are:

—Answering the phone
—Answering routine e-mail requests
—Sorting mail and opening it
—Filing
—Proofreading
—Updating mailing lists and other computer lists
—Preparing large mailings
—Ordering office supplies
—Publicizing your business
—Taking care of your taxes
—Handling payroll
—Running errands

Just because you can do everything yourself doesn't mean that you should. Delegating frees you to concentrate on the things you do best and enjoy the most. If you get rid of the tasks you find annoying or burdensome, you'll find you're actually more efficient at everything else—the other tasks don't bog you down and you're freed of the negative emotions that come when you persistently put something off. That's good time management.

Once you've gone through your list and decided what it is you are going to delegate, your next step is deciding who is to do the job. Telecommuters may have specific people to whom to turn. Others may have to seek out temp services, freelancers, or take a close look at family members to see who has the potential to get work done.

Here are some of the places to check for help:

- Independent mailing centers. These service businesses provide one-stop shopping for stationery supplies and postage stamps, but consider delegating to them as well. Ask that they pack up your packages, and let them make your photocopies and assemble presentation materials if need be.

- Office temporaries for everything from secretarial help to legal work. You're no different from a corporate office; if you need help, a temporary service allows you to add staff without the headaches of doing payroll and taxes.

- Outside professionals for payroll, publicity, marketing, accounting, etc. Look for professionals to help you out. Ask for referrals from other people who run businesses similar to yours, or read ads or check the Yellow Pages. If you phone someone from an ad or the Yellow Pages, be sure to ask for and check references.

- Qualified adults in your town who are looking for extra work. One homebased designer/marketing expert hired a retired woman in his neighborhood to help out with errands.

- Your kids or other people's kids. (Even if you have kids you may find it easier to get a few paid hours work out of someone else's child.) Hire them for errands, copying, collating, sorting, packing, shipping, envelope stuffing, almost anything you can imagine. Some may actually be capable of doing more than clerical tasks.

IT'S ALL IN THE TEACHING

Most people find it very difficult to delegate, and part of the problem is that they don't invest the time in showing anyone how they want the job done. Here's a method that will help you overcome this:

Step One: Training

—Explain the job.

—Even if a person has the basic idea of what is to be done, take the time to demonstrate exactly how you'd like the task performed.

—Work alongside the person, observing how he or she performs the task the first few times.

—Set a firm completion date. "As soon as possible . . ." puts most projects on the back burner.

—If the task is a lengthy one, establish steps with interim deadlines.

Step Two: Put It in Writing.

—Use index cards to note the task, the steps involved, the date assigned, and when you'd like it completed. Make two cards, give one to the person performing the task, and keep one in an index card box that you can use to keep track of what you've delegated.

—Record in your calendar when you need to follow up and when the task should be completed.

Step Three: Supervise

—Let the person know you're available if there are questions.

—Make it clear that you'd rather be informed along the way if there are problems; tell them not to wait until the last minute to let you know they ran into difficulties. Then if they do have a problem, don't rant or rave, scream or mutter, give dirty looks or chew their heads off.

—Don't hover. Even your children should be given some space to do a job on their own. (There's no quicker way to discourage help than having the "boss" stand over and make suggestions throughout.)

—When something goes wrong, show the person how to fix it. Don't openly criticize or snatch the project away.

At the conclusion of the task, pay the person promptly and praise them for a job well done.

K EEP IT SIMPLE

1. If you don't have an employee, turn to outside services for getting office work done.
2. The key to successful delegation is in the training. Take time to teach the job carefully. It will save you time in the long run.
3. Once you've delegated a task, don't hover.

PART SIX

PERSONAL ISSUES

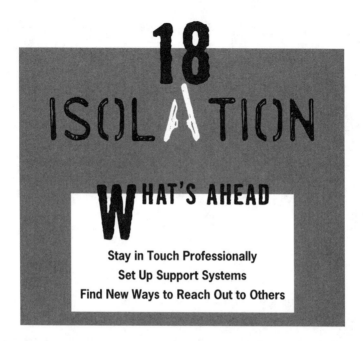

18

ISOLATION

WHAT'S AHEAD

Stay in Touch Professionally
Set Up Support Systems
Find New Ways to Reach Out to Others

Working from home can be lonely. Even if you have children and an active social life with other parents whom you see at the schoolyard, most people still need adult contact with other professionals in order to maintain a feeling of excitement for working at home.

To begin, you need to analyze the kind of work you do in order to establish how much "people" time you can afford. People who are responsible for creating a "product" (architects, writers, graphic artists, etc.) need a great deal of isolated office time in order to keep up production of the work, and therefore, they may need to limit the number of weekday lunches or meetings to just a few. Other types of workers may have less need for working alone. Consultants and anyone involved in any type of sales need to be out and about a good portion of the time. If you're in this line of work you must force yourself to keep up an active "people" schedule.

Here are suggestions for staying in touch with other pros:

STAY IN TOUCH PROFESSIONALLY

- Keep a list of people with whom you need to stay in touch. Make a point of scheduling lunches or appointments with these people on a regular basis.

- Join organizations. Anything from an industry group to the local Rotary, Chamber of Commerce, or Toastmasters Club can put you in touch with other businesspeople.

- Make a point to attend meetings of groups where you think you can do business (not just your own professional organizations).

- Host networking events at your home. With luck other people will follow your lead and you'll develop a relationship with a circle of people.

- Participate in joint ventures. If another entrepreneur has expertise that your client could use, consider bringing that person in on a job. Working together with another person gives you regular personal contact. (Collaborating on a book is an excellent example of two isolated businesspeople joining together to work on a common project.)

SET UP SUPPORT SYSTEMS

- Form a support group. The group can be as varied (working mothers in all types of jobs) or narrow (only artists) as you choose, and establish a schedule for getting together.
- Choose a phone buddy. The buddy needn't even be officially informed that he or she is serving in that capacity. A reciprocal phone arrangement may simply evolve for the two of you.

FIND NEW WAYS TO REACH OUT TO OTHERS

- Be active in your community. Serving on a town or school committee permits you to interact with people on a professional level, and this type of work is often a good social supplement to working at home all alone.

- Take classes in your field or explore new areas through course work. No matter what the subject, taking a class gets you out of the house and puts you in contact with other people on a regular basis.

- Reach out via the World Wide Web. While electronic networking isn't as good as personal contact, it does offer support groups and an easy way to feel connected and in touch with other people. The only problem is that it's so easy that some of my clients find they spend too much time online. Monitor your use just as you would monitor personal telephone time.

- While you do need to stay in touch with adults, don't discount the social value (and fun) of your kids if you have them. A lunch out or a walk to the park with the younger set will prove socially satisfying as well. (They may be short but they're still good company!)

KEEP IT SIMPLE

1. Even when it means time away from your desk, it's important to stay in contact with individuals and business groups who are a part of your industry.

2. Support groups, which can consist of people from many other

professions as well as your own, can be enormously helpful, as can a phone buddy.

3. Take courses, work in your community, and find other ways to stay involved with people. It will keep you energized.

19

WORKING FROM HOME WHEN YOU HAVE CHILDREN

WHAT'S AHEAD

Setting Ground Rules

The Ideal: Establishing Systems

The Reality: When the Lines Blur

Sick Days

School Holidays

Your Office as a Learning Experience

For many people, particularly women, children are one of the primary reasons they've decided to work at home. However, parents should be forewarned that the image of the baby sleeping for a long period of time or the toddler playing at your feet while you conduct business on the telephone is little more than a pipe dream. Once you start working from home you realize that babies don't sleep as much as you thought and the toddler views the telephone as Enemy #1 and will do all he can to create havoc while you're on it. Things don't get much better with age. Parents who work at home quickly realize that raising a family while working at home offers many advantages, but some basic systems and ground rules must be put in place if it's going to work.

Like any working parent, you may encounter questions from your children: "Why do you have to go to work?" or "Why do you have to work NOW?" Remember, you have a distinct advantage (and they do, too): By working from home you are providing a positive role model for your child, and chances are you're going to miss very little of their childhood now that your base is at home.

SETTING GROUND RULES

If you've always worked outside of the home and are now establishing a home office, take the following steps:

- Discuss with your children what this change will mean. While you will be nearby and available at times when you weren't before, make certain that your children understand that it doesn't mean you're constantly available to them.

- Talk to them about where you plan to locate your office, what hours you'll be working, and who will answer their needs when you're not available.

THE IDEAL: ESTABLISHING SYSTEMS

- Establish regular work hours to help family members understand your availability.

- Work with a closed door. Then you're less "tempting" to them.

- Hire someone to care for the children during the time you expect to work, or find a good day-care program for your children. When the children go to a day-care provider it offers structure to your days as well as theirs, and by having the children happily occupied outside the home, it reduces the likelihood that you'll be disturbed during the workday.

- If you hire someone to be in the house, train your child-care person carefully. Even the most experienced workers are generally accustomed to working in a home where the parents are gone, and they often have difficulty drawing the line. Make it clear that they are the "boss" while you are working, and that you won't second-guess the decisions they make during your work day. Also clarify under what circumstances you can be disturbed.

- Discuss emergencies. Start with the definition of one (one family says it has to be a "blood" emergency to qualify as a reason for bothering Mom), and talk about what to do in one. If you have household help or if your spouse is around, they should be the first line of defense in the event of an emergency. After that, of course, the home-based working parent is on call.

- Set rules about the use of the phone lines. "Children are not permitted to use the business line," and with older children, "Children are responsible for answering the home line" are two good ones.

- Pack your lunch and purchase an electric tea kettle for heating water for tea or coffee. If your children are home during the day and you emerge from your office, you're bound to be lured into a conversation you didn't want to have.

- Give your children a sense of when you'll next be available. If they are too young to tell time, use terms like "when it starts to get dark . . ." or some other way to describe when you'll reemerge from your office. If your children tell time, buy one of those clocks shop owners use on their front doors. Set it for the time when you intend to quit work that day.

THE REALITY: WHEN THE LINES BLUR

No matter what your resolve, there will be days when the sitter doesn't show up and you just *have* to get something done, or an unexpected phone call that you really need to take comes in after office hours. On those occasions, you need to figure out what you'll do about the children.

- If you've carpeted your office, you'll be glad. Children in an office are less easily heard if some of their activities are buffered by carpeting.

- Be sure your phone has a mute button. There's nothing worse than being on a conference call when the doorbell rings, the dog barks, and the kids come running through.

- Young elementary school children will enjoy having a work station (a small table and chair will do) in your office if you have the space. They'll be thrilled to be invited in to work at their desks while you file or handle a quick phone call.

- If you upgrade your computer in the near future, keep your old one. You can use it for staff if your business grows, and in the meantime, load it with a few games. That way your child can "work" along side you on occasion.

- Put away some videotapes. If you're confronting an imminent deadline and you're also in charge of the kids, you can achieve

20–60 minutes (depending on the age of the child) of peace by letting them watch a special tape.

- If you're in a pinch and have to bring a toddler or preschooler into your office for a short time, have an emergency activity bag (toys they haven't seen in a long time or a favorite coloring book and markers) that will amuse them for a time.

- Preschool and young elementary schoolers will enjoy "office" toys like a plastic telephone, a cash register, and some extra message pads.

Sick Days

Nothing wreaks havoc on a home-based worker's life more quickly than the words, "I don't feel good," spoken by a child with a flushed face. The likely trip to the pediatrician and tending to the child's needs during the day make home-based workers long for the structure of going to a "real" office. Here are some suggestions for coping:

- Once the pediatrician appointment is set, look at your calendar and "to do" list. What really needs to get done and what can be delayed? You may have to wait until evening when your spouse arrives home to cover for you, but you'll feel better if you've narrowed your day's goals down to only an item or two.

- Have in place a support system of people you can call if you're in a crunch. A nearby grandmother or a baby-sitter coming in for the morning might get you out of a bind.

- Consider the age of the child. A baby or toddler will likely demand your attention for the time he or she is awake, though there's nothing wrong with doing some low-level business reading while your toddler watches a television program or two. If you're lucky, your child will nap for a little while, giving you a break.

- Elementary school children might be happy settling in to your office for a little while. Help them plan out something to do and set a time limit for how long you need to work. Ask for "Quiet Time" and to hold all questions until you can give them your full attention. There's no better way to frazzle your own nerves than to try to get some work done while carrying on a conversation with an eight-year-old. Promise to do something special with your child (play Chinese checkers; do a puzzle; work on an art project) if she cooperates by amusing herself for a brief period of time.

- If your child is sick for a prolonged period, try to find someone to come in and help. In addition to needing the work time, you need the break from nonstop child-care. Your child will actually benefit from seeing a fresh face now and then. If this isn't feasible, then work out a schedule with your spouse so that you can reclaim some time for yourself to get done what you need to.

SCHOOL HOLIDAYS

While children eagerly await the 3 P.M. bell prior to a school holiday, most home-based workers feel like these days off come far too frequently—it's difficult to run a home-based business that doesn't need you on days other than school days.

- Resolve what your plans are for each holiday. The December holidays are generally a good time to kick back and relax. Close the office and don't even try to get anything done.

- Make a case by case decision for other holidays. A long Columbus Day weekend may feel just right to you, but in February you may be desperate to get work done.

- When you are trying to work and they are at home, give them a specific time when you'll be finished.

- If you do need to work, make very specific plans for the children. You may be able to find a morning gymnastics program for the week (some places that offer after-school programs also schedule "camps" for vacation weeks). Schedule playdates, and plan to take at least one day off to do something with your kids. If their other time has been filled nicely, then you'll all look forward to the event you plan as a special family time together.

YOUR OFFICE AS A LEARNING EXPERIENCE

While a great deal of this discussion focuses on how to keep your office and your children separate, it's also important to recognize that you are serving as a positive role model for your children. When they see you exert self-discipline to get into your office on beautiful days when the beach would be a lot more fun, you're showing them that being industrious is an admirable form of behavior. And when they absorb the small bits and pieces of what you do in your line of work, it may interest or inspire them in ways you'll never know.

What's more, with a little creativity from you, you can teach them a little about running an office, and you'll find this will be a help to you, too:

- Think of age-appropriate tasks your children could do:
    —Count merchandise

    —Pack products

    —Type labels

    —Help with simple jobs like stuffing envelopes or stapling

    —Organize supplies
- Older children could take phone messages and even process orders for you.
- Pay your children for the time they spend working for you.

(You can, however, distinguish between the times when they are truly of assistance to you and the times when you've made up something for them to do so that you can work for a few more minutes.) If they are earning more than a couple of dollars here and there, talk to your accountant. This is a legitimate business expense.

- Taking an older child on a business trip with you can be a fun way of spending time together while showing him or her a little more of the country. Be certain that you can either leave your child with a relative or friend when you're busy working or keep your child with you if you're attending meetings. A teenager is old enough to be on his own in a hotel room for brief periods of time.

K EEP IT SIMPLE

1. Establish a regular child-care system that permits you the workday you need.

2. Create support systems that you can put into effect during school vacations or sick days.

3. When all else fails and you've got to tend to your family's needs, look at your calendar and "to do" list and select what *must* be done and what can wait.

20

WHEN TWO WORK FROM HOME

WHAT'S AHEAD

Co-Existing Without Driving Each Other Crazy

The Ground Rules

Two at Home in a Single Business

The Perks

I was having coffee at a restaurant one morning when I overheard an interesting conversation. A thirtyish daughter was telling an older woman—almost certainly her mother—how she was encouraging her husband, who was starting his own business, to work from home. It was clear from the conversation that the young woman already had some type of home-based enterprise, and I had to laugh—the look on the older woman's face clearly read: "Are you nuts?" as she mouthed the words, "Keep your mouth shut!"

Maintaining a strong and happy marriage is often made more challenging when both of you are working from home full or part-time.

Some spouses run totally separate home businesses; others are united in running a family business. This chapter discusses some of the stresses that can occur in either arrangement.

CO-EXISTING WITHOUT DRIVING EACH OTHER CRAZY

Many home-based couples with this arrangement make a point of providing as much separation as possible:

- Create space for two separate home offices. The at-home writer is going to be miserable sharing space with a spouse who is making sales calls. The person with the greatest need for working uninterrupted should have the office that is the most removed from the center of the household.

- Try to place shared business equipment in a large closet or hallway that is accessible to both without disturbing each other. A fax machine or copier located in either of your offices will be annoying when the other person comes in to use it.

- Install separate business telephone lines and separate modem lines to reduce friction over use of the household communication systems. Specify what you're to do about phone coverage. Will either of you answer the home line during the day, or do you plan to cover it with a machine during working hours? There's nothing more annoying than a phone line that rings and rings, or being forced to answer it because the person who has agreed to answer it doesn't seem to be doing so.

- Discuss schedules generally. Do you want to take a morning walk together before starting work? Do you want to have lunch together occasionally or always? If so, at what time? Who is going to fix it? (One spouse shouldn't have to be responsible for the midday meals of the other.)

- Discuss schedules specifically. In the morning, find out what the other has planned for the day. That way you'll know who is going to be out on appointments and who is working at home on any given day.

THE GROUND RULES

- Discuss money. If one of you is just starting a business this may mean a change in income for the family so discuss and plan out a new budget to help reduce stress.

- Discuss chores and divide them fairly. Try not to assign home responsibilities based on who makes more money. While the major breadwinner will, of course, need to maintain his or her job responsibilities, the person with the new business shouldn't be burdened with all house and child-care responsibilities. If so, it makes it so much more difficult for the new business to grow so that it eventually will be more lucrative.

- Discuss the children, if any live at home. What are the issues that concern them? Who does the carpooling? Who copes with sick days? These issues will be handled more smoothly if they are discussed ahead of time.

- Talk about talking. Many people wander around while thinking. Establish ground rules for working uninterrupted (even when it looks like you're not working). One client reports that she's still working (thinking) when she stands up to stretch her legs after an hour or so at the computer. She may go to the kitchen for a cup of tea, and so long as no one stops her on the way back to her office, she finds this use of time very productive. Spouses need to know how not to interfere with this process for each other.

TWO AT HOME IN A SINGLE BUSINESS

Many couples find it exhilarating to build a business together, but it does require thought and maintenance to keep both the business and the marriage alive.

- If both of you are working toward the same business goals it can be very exciting but also stressful. First thing you know, sales figures become the focus of dinner and become pillow talk as well.

- Clearly define your business as well as your personal roles. When working together in two capacities you need to be certain you've agreed about who does what.

- Don't talk business after hours. Couples need to distance themselves from the business some of the time to make certain that they maintain a family life and a personal life that is not contingent on how well the business is doing.

- Involve your kids in meaningful ways. A family business is a fact of life for the family, including the kids. Use it as an opportunity to teach the kids about business, about commitment, and about family.

THE PERKS

- Make dates with each other. Plan to go to lunch together at a new restaurant or take an afternoon off and visit the local art museum or have family time with the kids. This is one of the best benefits of working from home.

- Develop some shared hobbies as well as separate ones. While there's nothing better than having a tennis partner available for a 3 P.M. match on Fridays, you want to be certain that each of you develops a separate set of friends and interests so that you go off to do things on your own and bring back new friends and expanded interests.

KEEP IT SIMPLE

1. Establish separate space for each person, and place jointly shared equipment in common space whenever possible.

2. Discuss everything from errands and child care to phone coverage so that the ground rules are very clear.

3. Don't talk business after hours. It's important to maintain a life that is separate from your work so that you both have the opportunity to relax and to develop separate interests.

PART SEVEN

YOUR

TRAVELING

HOME OFFICE

21
A WELL-PACKED BRIEFCASE

I know a "practical" successful man who must have the world's largest collection of briefcases. Every time he goes to a business conference, he's thrilled to receive a "designer special," a carryall with the company's logo boldly imprinted on the front. This self-made gentleman believes he's set for life with a tote for any occasion. And when one wears out all he needs to do is dip into his collection for another style, certainly a cost-effective way to acquire briefcases. His basic philosophy? "No one has ever not done business with me because of the briefcase I carry. Style comes from within. Your briefcase is just an accessory, not who you are."

A briefcase is still a much-needed business tool. It's important to select a bag that is manageable, and pack it well so that you know you have everything with you. In addition, using your briefcase properly will make a difference in managing your time.

CHOOSING THE RIGHT BAG

Here are the elements to look for when choosing a briefcase:

- A lightweight bag that zips or snaps closed to keep out rain or snow. I prefer soft-sided bags to hard cases. The suitcase-like cases can get heavy and are a little more awkward to carry.

- An "all weather" case. In a storm your papers won't get soaked. Stay away from materials that don't hold up over time, show stains, and don't wipe clean.

- Detachable shoulder strap. While you may not always want the extra strap, it makes the bag much easier to carry when traveling.

- Exterior pocket for newspaper and umbrella.

- Interior pockets (the more the better) for supplies. You can substitute by using small zippered pouches (preferably transparent) if necessary.

- Some women find it more convenient to let a briefcase double as a pocketbook so they needn't carry two bags. To stay organized, add a zippered pouch to hold money, credit cards, toiletries, and tissues.

ON-THE-GO ITEMS

- Here are the "must-haves":

  —Calendar and address book or personal digital assistant to keep track of your schedule and/or any people whom you need to reach while you're out of the office

  —Business cards

  —Pad of paper

  —Pens, pencils, highlighter. Always carry more than one pen and pencil. If someone borrows one or you lose one during the day, you still have a spare.

  —Reading material or paperwork for idle moments.

- Depending on the nature of your work and the length of time you'll be out of your office, here's a list of items to make your life easier:

—Office tools such as scissors, tape dispenser, small stapler, rubber bands, and a ruler

—Sticky-backed notepad

—Stamps

—Calculator

—Clip-it tool for cutting out articles

—Minicassette recorder for taking notes

—Safety pins for fastening a hem or holding a loose button

—Tissues

—Moist towelettes

—Toothbrush/dental floss

—Small amount of loose change

—Extra collar stays and socks for men, or pantyhose for women

—Medical kit (a few adhesive strips, pain reliever, allergy medicine, antacid tablets).

Be selective about what you put in your bag, or your case will be too heavy. (If you primarily travel by car, pack some of these items in a separate bag or container, creating a mobile office without having to carry it all in your briefcase. See Chapter 23.)

STAYING ORGANIZED WHILE OUT OF THE OFFICE

- There are several tips for being certain you leave with everything you need for a day:

  —As soon as you know you'll be visiting a company or an organization for a meeting, establish a file, which can be kept in your "Tickler" file, for what you will need for that meeting. As the days go by, put any paper you might need directly into this file.

  —If you'll be leaving early in the morning, pack your briefcase the day before so you can pack and organize everything you need.

  —Leave a note on top of your case listing any items that need to be packed at the last minute.

- The papers within your briefcase should all be stored within labeled file folders or envelopes ("Mail to Read," "Action," "To File," etc.).

- If your briefcase has two distinct compartments, designate a "to do" side and a "done" side. When you get back to the office, you've already begun the sorting process.

- Pack a #10 envelope in your briefcase, and use it to hold receipts for business expenses.

- When you call in for telephone messages, note them in your calendar, or enter them into your personal digital assistant. When you get back to the office you'll have a complete list of the people whom you need to call.

- Instead of writing ideas on scraps of paper and dropping them into the bottom of your bag, note them on extra pages of your calendar, enter them into your electronic organizer, or establish a small notebook on which you keep track of this type of information. When you get back to the office, add these items to your "Master List." (See Chapter 8.)

- When you get back to the office, be certain to empty your briefcase completely, sorting as you go. Items left in the briefcase for more than a day can easily be forgotten.

KEEP IT SIMPLE

1. Choose a lightweight, weatherproof bag that zips closed so that the items in your briefcase will be protected in all types of weather.

2. Take what you need but not more than you need. If you travel by car, put some of the items you might normally put in your briefcase (office tools, minicassette machine, medical kit) in a separate bag that can remain in your car.

3. Don't dump things into your briefcase during the day. Have with you file folders ("Action," "To File," etc.) and envelopes for receipts so that you can sort the papers as you put them in. This will save you time when you return to your office.

22

THE CAR: YOUR MOBILE OFFICE

WHAT'S AHEAD

Setting Up Your Mobile Office
Safety First
Car Basics
Car Organizers
Don't Leave Home Without:
Protecting What's Yours
Keeping Track of Mileage

If you travel for business by car, then you know the difference between getting out of a well-organized car and one that's a mess:

- Worker A is neat at home but her car's a disaster. She makes sales calls in the family minivan. When she arrives at her destination and opens the back hatch of the car a soccer ball rolls out of the trunk area. After retrieving it from the parking lot, she finds that her sales presentation materials, neatly placed in file folders when she left home, have been slipping around in the back of the car during the trip and have mixed in with the kids' snack wrappers and an empty juice box. Would she dare take a client to lunch in the car? Preferably not, unless the client wants golden fur from the family's Labrador on his suit, and he may need to push aside sports equipment and a backpack or two to get into the car.

- Worker B also has a family and drives a minivan, but she has decided to turn her car into a mobile office. She has a plastic container in the back of her car with office supplies; a portable file holds extra literature, letterhead, and some files; and items she'll need for the day are carefully packed in her briefcase. She gets the car cleaned every week or two to be certain there are no remnants of kids' snacks or lunches littering the floor, and she always carries a lint brush to be certain that when she steps out of the car she looks first rate.

Here's how to make your car complement the way you do business.

SETTING UP YOUR MOBILE OFFICE

- To keep papers neatly sorted, purchase a plastic portable file box that closes easily and will fit in the back of your car. Papers won't slip out, and odds and ends won't fall in.

- Within your file box, place several file folders for holding papers. Keep stationery and envelopes for on-the-road letters, and take along a folder labeled "To File," and "To Do on Return." The other folders should hold what is appropriate for your business. One salesperson makes certain he has copies of all sales literature so he never runs out and never has to mail papers back to a client afterward.

- Office life on the road is easier if you have handy tools like a stapler, scissors, adhesive-backed notes, and an extra box of pens with you. Refer to Chapter 21 about briefcases. Those who travel mainly by car (not public transportation) can lighten their briefcase load by storing many of their supplies in the car rather than on their shoulder or back.

- A cellular phone is vital if you're on the road for long stretches. Refer to Chapter 10 for complete information.

- If you're on the road a lot, consider an in-car fax. You can purchase a machine that attaches to your cellular or portable telephone with a special jack. The machine runs on battery power or can be plugged into your cigarette lighter.

SAFETY FIRST

- At some point most businesspeople need to make calls from the road, but the statistics for car accidents increase for those who insist on dialing and driving. You have three options to increase safety:

  1. If you need to make a call, pull over (or get off at the next exit if you're on the highway), and make the call while the car is stopped.

  2. Have a passenger dial for you and put the phone on "speaker" if that's possible.

  3. Invest in a car phone system with voice-activated dialing and a speakerphone. While not phoning while driving is the safest course of action, this system at least keeps your hands on the wheel.

- Have next to you a minicassette or small dictaphone for recording notes about your latest brainstorm or what you want to do based on any telephone conversation. Trying to write notes about a conversation while driving is difficult to do and can be dangerous.

- You might also consider the latest in technology, speech recognition digital recorders that let you dictate notes that are quickly converted to editable text once you're back at your PC.

CAR BASICS

- Take good care of your car. Get on a regular maintenance schedule to reduce the likelihood of being waylaid by a breakdown.

- Register with the Automobile Association of America (AAA). Just when you least expect it, you'll discover you've left the keys in the car, a tire is flat, or your car won't start, and it's nice to know that AAA will come to your rescue. (This is when a car phone comes in handy!)

- Be sure to have with you important car documents (registration, insurance card). Place these papers in a protective envelope and store it in the glove compartment.

- Also have with you maps of the area in which you're driving along with a pocket flashlight or lighted magnifier for night driving. (Unless you've got eyes like an eagle, reading a map by the car overhead light can be more than challenging.) Some luxury cars are now being created with a built-in electronic road map that provides verbal directions to your destination.

These computer programs will become more commonplace in cars later on, and in all likelihood, the prices will go down.

- Every car should also be equipped for emergencies: a flashlight, a first aid kit, white handkerchief for using as a distress signal, flares, a tire jack, tools, some bottled water, and a blanket should all be stored in a canvas bag in the trunk.

- Keep a spare key for your car in your wallet so that you're never caught without a key.

CAR ORGANIZERS

- Purchase a caddy designed to hold books on tape and/or CDs. That way all your listening materials are well organized.

- For writing notes once parked, many people like the notepad and pen with suction cup that attaches to the dashboard.

- A pocket organizer that hangs on the back of one of the front seats of the car can help you keep family paraphernalia neat or provide storage for extra maps and a flashlight.

DON'T LEAVE HOME WITHOUT:

- Spare change for parking, and money or a "pass" for getting through tolls. (Some states now have a computer billing system where cards displaying an electronic "pass" don't need to stop to pay the toll. This is highly convenient for drivers and a real time-saver.)

- Supply of paper towels for spills or those unavoidable meals in the car.

- Box of tissues.

- Car wastebasket or plastic bags that can be tossed out.

- Folding umbrella.

- Window scraper in winter; a window cover in summer.

PROTECTING WHAT'S YOURS

- Equipment should be stored out of sight. Locking it in a car trunk is ideal. If you drive a minivan or a sports utility vehicle without a trunk, keep a blanket in the car to throw over anything that might be easily visible.

- Be sure you're insured for what you're carrying. Items that are attached to the car will be covered by a car insurance policy; items that are not attached (fax machine, portable phone) must be covered under your homeowner's policy. Check your policies' limits and deductibles to make sure that your equipment is properly insured. If necessary, you purchase the appropriate rider.

KEEPING TRACK OF MILEAGE

Careful record-keeping is very important if you plan to claim mileage on your income tax return. You can:

- Record mileage in your palmtop computer or directly onto your planner.
- Keep a small notebook and pen in your glove compartment, expressly for recording mileage. It gives you all the mileage information in one place, and you needn't flip through other calendar notations in order to find the mileage information at tax time.

KEEP IT SIMPLE

1. Set up a mobile office for your car, complete with file folders, desk supplies, and stationery and envelopes. Store these things in a portable file box you can leave in the back of your car.

2. To make calls from the road, make safety a priority. Pull over to call, let a passenger dial for you, or invest in a phone system with voice-activated dialing and a speakerphone.

3. Keep your car in good repair. There's nothing that will inconvenience you more than a breakdown on the way to or from a business meeting.

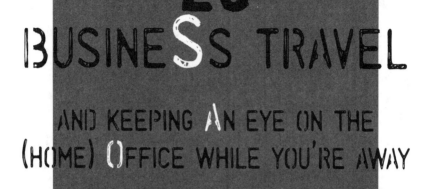

23

BUSINESS TRAVEL

AND KEEPING AN EYE ON THE (HOME) OFFICE WHILE YOU'RE AWAY

WHAT'S AHEAD

Smooth Departures
Packing
Packing Paperwork
Trip Preparations
The Trip
On Arrival
Your Return

Leaving your home office for a business trip is simpler today because of all the technological ways you can stay in touch.

While there's no doubt that packing up and leaving home still stirs up a certain degree of stress, there are ways to simplify both the "departure" and the "staying in touch" even for the home-based worker.

SMOOTH DEPARTURES

- If you travel regularly, have a standing arrangement with a travel agent so that someone else can take charge of getting you there and getting you home. Your agent should also know what seat to request and what type of meal to order. While you can book the flight yourself by phone or via the Internet, home office workers are generally wearing so many "hats" (doing so many jobs) that it's nice to get help when you can.

- Talk to the travel agent or check with the airlines regarding the best ways to earn mileage and/or how to schedule your stay in order to save money.

- Go over your current work assignments, anticipating and resolving what problems you can. Make contingency plans for any pending items when you leave.

- If you have staff, delegate work they can do for you.

- Frequent travelers should prepare a "While I'm Away" list for anyone at home or in the office, and a "last-minute reminders" checklist. That way you simply update it each time you go away.

- Prepare an itinerary of your travel plans, complete with phone numbers and flight information. Give a copy to those who might need to get hold of you.

- Let major clients know you plan to be gone so your absence doesn't catch them by surprise.

- Change your voice mail message. While you needn't say you're out of town, provide helpful information for your callers such as what time you'll be checking in for messages.

- Though voice mail and e-mail will keep you in touch with many people, see what you can do about the U.S. mail. If you don't have staff, will another family member be at home to watch for anything important? If not, does it make sense to talk to a neighbor about checking your mail? Or you can have it held at the post office until you return.

- If you're leaving the household empty, consider what to do about the newspapers. If no one can pick them up for you, cancel delivery temporarily.

- If you're leaving kids at home, give them a copy of your itinerary as well as a rundown of their schedule while you're away. Leave emergency telephone numbers for the person in charge, and arrange a time to call in regularly so that they can count on when they'll hear from you. A calendar countdown and tape recordings of their favorite stories help ease the pain of your absence for little ones; older ones will enjoy receiving e-mail from you.

PACKING

- Invest in a lightweight piece of carry-on luggage with wheels. If you don't have to check your bag at the airport, it will save you a great deal of time. When shopping:

  —Check to be certain it qualifies as "carry on." Airlines are getting tough about this so ask the travel store to verify that it is an appropriate size.

  —Lift it; even with wheels there will be times when you need to pick up the bag. You don't want one that is too heavy or too bulky when empty.

  —Note pocket placement. Are they well-placed?

  —Check convenience. Each person has different packing needs (packing a suit jacket is very different from packing a long skirt) so be certain that this bag will hold what you need when traveling for a day or two or more.

  —Try the handle. Ideal handles pull up easily and quickly with the push of an on-handle button.

- If you must take a bag that will be checked, label it on the outside with only your name and a telephone number so that no one who sees the label will know where you live (and realize you're traveling). Place your business card within for complete identification. Unless you have a particularly distinctive bag, tie a colored ribbon on the handle of the bag to make it easier to spot as it comes off the carousel.

- If your bag is checked, pack a carry-on with essentials in case your bag is lost.

- Everyone should have a permanently packed toiletries bag with travel toothbrush and paste, razor, comb, lotion, etc., all ready to go.

- Pack a travel medicine kit as well. In a separate zippered pouch, pack pain reliever tablets, antacid tablets, anti-diarrheal medicine, adhesive strips, cough drops, decongestant, and any prescription, medicines or vitamins you might need.

- Economy-size products are perfect for travel. When you get home from a trip simply restock anything on which you're running low.

- Stock up on other small, lightweight items that can also remain permanently packed: travel clock, shower cap, travel hair dryer, steamer, wash-up towelettes, collapsible plastic skirt or pants hanger, lint brush, stain remover, and sewing kit.

- If you don't already have one, create a packing checklist.

—To plan out what you'll need, write down the days you'll be gone and then make a list of the clothing you'll need for each event. Select clothing with a basic color scheme that will coordinate to make several outfits, and plan to layer in order to adjust for the temperature.

—Create an "evergreen" list of items such as socks, underwear, belts, sunglasses, running shoes, etc., so that you needn't write down the basics each time. (These are also the items easiest to forget.)

• For most people, losing their glasses on a trip would be a major problem. If you have a pair of glasses you can spare, leave them permanently packed in your bag. That way if you ever lose your glasses, you've already got a backup. If you don't have an extra pair handy, take along a copy of your prescription. If you have to you can get a new pair made up on your trip.

Packing PAPERWORK

• Pack your briefcase with your trip in mind. Take along:

1. All information needed for your business meetings, but don't take entire client files unless you'll really need them.

2. Any files pertaining to other issues that might arise while you're away. If you know Client A is having some difficul-

ties and may need your help; pop relevant papers into your briefcase.

3. A special file for work-related information gathered on the trip. Two #10 envelopes will also come in handy. Use one for business cards collected while you're away, and one for receipts (as you drop receipts into the envelope, write on the back what you were paying for).

4. A file with a few pieces of your letterhead stationery, envelopes, and a supply of stamps. That way if you need to mail off a letter while on the road you're fully equipped.

5. Extra pens.

6. Work to get done on the flight.

7. Add a magazine or a novel for leisure reading.

• Pack a permanent travel kit for your computer as well. If you don't already know what you need, visit your local computer shop and discuss what equipment you have and what you need in order to be able to access your e-mail and the Internet while traveling. There are so many new gadgets being developed that, depending on the equipment you are using, there may be something new that's perfect for your needs. Get the toll-free technical support number to take along with you in case you need hookup advice.

TRIP PREPARATIONS

- Get a current copy of the OAG pocket flight guide. (Official Airline Guides, 2000 Clearwater Drive, Oak Brook, IL 60521-9953; 708-574-6000.) If you have a schedule change or a problem with your flight, you can quickly map out a new schedule yourself.

- Advance research will determine which rental car company has the best reputation for price and customer service. Apply for "membership." This will speed your time getting out of the airport.

- If you're traveling overseas, arrange to get appropriate foreign currency in advance.

- If you frequently travel to the same city on business, start a file where you can keep relevant information, everything from business groups and contact information to subway maps and tourist sites to visit.

- Look for hotels that cater to businesspeople. They'll have executive floors with in-room faxes, express check-in and checkout and benefits such as free newspapers and coffee or tea. Also investigate whether the hotel has a "frequent guest" program. You may be eligible for some "perks" if you sign on to stay in one hotel or with one chain regularly.

- Consider investing in a membership in an airline club if you're a frequent traveler. It gives you a pleasant place to relax or do business if your flight is delayed. If you don't join a club, some airports have business centers where you can work.

- Some credit card companies offer a concierge-style service for their premium card holders. If you travel a great deal it may be worth paying for this extra level of service.

THE TRIP

- Be sure you have with you your passport or driver's license for identification at the airport.

- Have on hand dollar bills for tipping and coins and a phone card or cell phone for calls.

- Put written confirmation of your hotel reservation in a convenient place so that you can produce it if necessary.

- Use flight time for taking care of office matters, preparing for the meeting you're attending, or working on projects you brought from home.

ON ARRIVAL

- Ask the rental car company to provide you with computerized directions to your destination.

- Unpack as soon as you check into your room. Shake out your clothing, and if anything needs to be pressed your travel steamer will come in handy, particularly for suits.

- Place your breakfast order with room service the night before to save time in the morning.

- Consider what the concierge can do for you and make good use of that service. Tickets, dinner reservations, and even a meeting room can usually all be worked out by the concierge and this will minimize some of the stress of traveling.

- Call in to voice mail and check your e-mail regularly while you're away. You don't want to come home to a backlog or any surprises.

- If you're gone for a prolonged period of time and someone is monitoring your mail, ask that they send the more important items by overnight delivery. This lets you process some of what's coming in while you're away.

- Try to take care of any paperwork generated by your trip so that you'll have less to do when you return.

- If you have any break in your business routine, treat yourself to something fun to do. A workout at the hotel gym, sightseeing, shopping, a visit to an art museum, or dinner at a great restaurant will all give you a well-deserved break in the work routine.

YOUR RETURN

- Set aside at least an hour of uninterrupted time to go through the mail or handle any issues that came up while you were away.
- Organize your "To Do" pile by priority.
- Gather any work and reading material that can be polished off in short time slots during the day and carry this work with you.
- Review your calendar and make any needed changes.
- Establish a time when you'll return all telephone calls to people you need to reach.

KEEP IT SIMPLE

1. Planning ahead for business travel will help take the stress out of it. Have a basic packing list for yourself, and a "While I'm Away"

checklist for those at home. Amend them as necessary depending on the circumstances of each trip.

2. When it comes to paperwork, pack the files you'll need for the trip itself and also take along any files you might need for "client emergencies."

3. Stay in touch by e-mail and voice mail, and keep up with your paperwork, organizing it neatly within your briefcase throughout the trip. That way you'll be able to hit the ground running when you get home.

PART EIGHT

THE

FUTURE

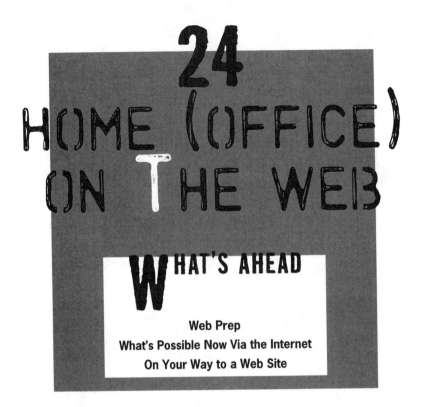

24

HOME (OFFICE) ON THE WEB

WHAT'S AHEAD

Web Prep
What's Possible Now Via the Internet
On Your Way to a Web Site

The Internet is the best thing that ever happened to home businesses. Whether you're located on a ranch in Dakota or an apartment in New York City, you now have resources available to you that you never could have dreamed of, and your outreach can be far beyond what you'd ever thought it would be. More and more business is going to be occurring on the Internet and via the Internet. Suffice it to say that Internet mastery should become a priority right now.

What's on the Web and what's possible via the Web are changing daily, but regardless of these changes, there are specific steps you can take to prepare.

WEB PREP

- Whenever you gather customer information, request an e-mail address as well as the traditional request for street address and phone number. Notifying customers of new products or special sales is faster, cheaper, and easier using e-mail.

- Make certain your e-mail address is in all your promotional information. Even without a Web site you'll find that customers are happy to zap off an e-mail requesting information or asking questions.

- To learn more about what's going on on the Internet, start visiting Web sites for all types of businesses. It will give you an idea of what works and what doesn't.

WHAT'S POSSIBLE NOW VIA THE INTERNET

- Use e-mail as a customer reminder system. You can help increase their loyalty to you by keeping them abreast of what's going on with their account.

- Send your customers a regular "e-newsletter" to keep your name uppermost in their minds.

- Send documents by e-mail for online delivery.

- Contact the media. If you sell nationally, you can now read the *Detroit News*, the *Denver Post*, and the *Chicago Tribune* online. Get to know their reporters by reading the stories, and then contact them via e-mail with appropriate story ideas.

- Research online. You can do anything from product searches to market research online. This will save most business owners hours of time.

- Cut down on clutter. Because you know you can go online for the latest statistics on anything from traffic accidents to art theft, you no longer need to save that type of information in your paper files.

- Use online calendar and reminder systems.

- Hold a meeting online or establish collaborative work space for you and anyone you know, regardless of where they are located. (This is fully explained in Chapter 16.)

- Save time by arranging for pickups and tracking packages via the Web sites of major package delivery services.

- Fax. Some Internet services will send the document you e-mail them to someone else's fax machine where it will appear as a fax.

- Join "associate programs" to increase your sales reach.

- Shop and price shop for everything from digital cameras to office chairs.

ON YOUR WAY TO A WEB SITE

- If you don't yet have a Web site, consider teaming up with someone who does. You can test the waters for your products, and in all likelihood you'll be ready to mount your own Web site soon.

The Internet is going to be a great tool for home businesses. Never before has so much been so accessible and so inexpensive, and the fact that the Web increases our "people" outreach is not only good for business but it helps fight off loneliness as well. Start learning as much as you can now—you'll never look back.

KEEP IT SIMPLE

1. Start gathering customer e-mail addresses, and begin giving out your own e-mail address as well by putting it on your letterhead and brochures and handing it out freely.

2. Start learning by going on the Internet whenever you have time. You'll learn of new services and products, and you'll get ideas about what makes a good Web site.

3. If you don't have a Web site, experiment by teaming up with someone who does.

PART NINE

HOME OFFICE

CHEAT SHEET

When you're short on time and want to pick up a few tips on organizing your home office, you can cheat by turning directly to this section:

THE BUSINESS SIDE OF ESTABLISHING A HOME OFFICE

1. It's vital that you investigate the legalities of operating a home business in your neighborhood. If you try to skirt the law, the neighbors may trip you up.

2. When it comes to deliveries or parking by clients or employees, be considerate of the neighbors.

3. Call your insurance agent and describe what you're doing. Be sure that you have the proper coverage in the amount you need.

IDENTIFYING YOUR SPACE NEEDS

1. Consider your workstyle, your equipment needs, and your environmental preferences when selecting the optimum location for your home office.

2. Give the space a test run before making any major household changes.

3. If space for meeting with clients is a problem, remember that it's easy enough, often ideal, to meet clients at their own offices or in a hotel lobby. (This type of arrangement has the added benefit of leaving you in control of when the meeting ends.)

FURNITURE FOR THE HOME OFFICE

1. Choose your desk carefully based on where you plan to put your computer, how much surface space you want, and what type of drawers are practical for your work.
2. If space is at a premium, consider what office items you could place elsewhere in the house.
3. List all the other furniture, equipment or special areas (visitor waiting area?), and plan accordingly.

CREATING A COMFORTABLE LAYOUT

1. When laying out your office, place your desk first, and put it where you'll have access to the storage and the equipment you'll use every day.
2. Develop a lighting plan that provides consistent lighting through-

out your office. Eyes become fatigued when they have to keep readjusting to different light levels.

3. Paint the office before you move everything into it. If you use your home office regularly, you'll appreciate a nice paint job.

SETTING UP SHOP WITH THE RIGHT EQUIPMENT

1. Invest in the most powerful computer with the largest memory that you can afford. This will make it easier to update.

2. Store manuals, diskettes, and tech support numbers somewhere accessible where you can get your hands on them in a hurry.

3. When it comes to your computer, back up, back up, back up.

CALENDARS

1. Select the calendar style that's right for you and use only that one calendar.

2. Plan out your day the night before. Write down all appointments and record a complete "to do" list.

3. Be sure to check your calendar daily!

THE MASTER LIST/OFFICE NOTEBOOK

1. Record all "to do" items on one Master List. Your daily "to do" list will be culled from this running list.

2. Mark priority items with an asterisk and note due dates for projects that have them.

3. Set aside ten minutes at the end of your day to plan your next day's "to do" list. Schedule only 75 percent of your day so that you can cope with the unexpected.

GETTING WORK DONE

1. Establish a regular structure to your work pattern in order to better manage your time.

2. View projects as a series of steps, and identify exactly what it is you need to get done on any given day.

3. Don't wait for a big block of time in which to get work done. Start using small chunks of time, and you'll be surprised at what you can accomplish in 5-, 15-, and 30-minute blocks of time.

THE TELEPHONE

1. Evaluate what phone services you need, and consider whether you need a cellular phone or beeper (or both), and then shop carefully for them. Keep up with new developments—you may learn of additional developments that will be of great value to you.

2. Screen incoming calls when you're busy, and organize yourself prior to making outgoing calls so that the time you spend on the phone is used efficiently.

3. Learn how to end a call gracefully by using various "closing lines" indicating you've got to get off the phone.

FIGHTING INTERRUPTIONS AND DISTRACTIONS

1. Establish a regular interruption-free time for some of your work by getting up early, blocking out calls, or anything else you need to do that lets you work uninterrupted for a time.

2. Control interruptions by grouping those that you can anticipate and minimizing those that occur unexpectedly.

3. Resist the temptation to self-interrupt or to be lured away from

---

your work by the refrigerator, the family, or by a friend on the phone. Self-discipline is the key to getting things done.

PROCRASTINATION

1. Make a list of the items on which you're procrastinating, and evaluate which really need to be done and which can be crossed off without ever doing them.

2. If you're really having trouble getting something done, then you need help getting started. Break the project down into parts, and work on the project for just ten minutes.

3. Learn to say no to things you really don't like to do.

PROCESSING INCOMING INFORMATION

1. Establish a specific time for going through the mail, and try to process as much of it as you can in that one sitting.

2. Do the same with e-mail; check it at preplanned times, and handle incoming messages in order of priority, based on who it's from or what the headline is. (People waste an enormous amount of time by checking their e-mail too frequently.)

3. Try to reduce the amount of mail and e-mail you receive. Cancel subscriptions to magazines you don't have time to read, ask to be removed from catalog and direct mail mailing lists, and on the Internet, try to stay off the joke and other e-mail lists.

YOUR NEW FILING SYSTEM

1. Purchase real file cabinets if you don't already have them, and take the time to create a filing system that fits your needs.
2. Keep up with your filing, tossing as much as you can.
3. Action or Tickler files are the best way to keep track of ongoing projects and items on which you need to follow up.

THE ONGOING BATTLE AGAINST CLUTTER

1. Schedule time to clear out past clutter. Go through each paper and toss, act on it, or file it. You'll find that much of what is in this pile can go in the trash, so the work will go faster than you might expect.
2. Keep four "active" file folders near your desk: for papers to be copied, papers to be filed, papers with information that needs to

be entered into your computer, and a final file for reading material. Then schedule time regularly for working your way through the tasks in these files.

3. Start a file for all new projects, and note the task in your Office Notebook. That way you can put the papers away but still be reminded of the work you need to do.

MEETINGS

1. Make certain that any in-person meeting you schedule is necessary and cannot be accomplished by a telephone call, a "chat room" meeting, or a video conference.

2. Organize in advance for any type of meeting. Prepare an agenda, and create a file where you can put papers you will need for the meeting.

3. Start your meetings on time; keep people focused; and have someone take notes. Follow up afterwards by fax or by e-mail with any tasks that need to be done.

GETTING HELP

1. If you don't have an employee, turn to outside services for getting office work done.

2. The key to successful delegation is in the training. Take time to teach the job carefully. It will save you time in the long run.

3. Once you've delegated a task, don't hover.

I SOLATION

1. Even when it means time away from your desk, it's important to stay in contact with individuals and business groups who are a part of your industry.

2. Support groups, which can consist of people from many other professions as well as your own, can be enormously helpful, as can a phone buddy.

3. Take courses, work in your community, and find other ways to stay involved with people. It will keep you energized.

WORKING FROM HOME WHEN YOU HAVE CHILDREN

1. Establish a regular childcare system that permits you the workday you need.

2. Create support systems that you can put into effect during school vacations or sick days.

3. When all else fails and you've got to tend to your family's needs, look at your calendar and "to do" list and select what *must* be done and what can wait.

WHEN TWO WORK FROM HOME

1. Establish separate space for each person and place jointly shared equipment in common space whenever possible.

2. Discuss everything from errands and child care to phone coverage so that the ground rules are very clear.

3. Don't talk business after hours. It's important to maintain a life that is separate from your work so that you both have the opportunity to relax and to develop separate interests.

A WELL-PACKED BRIEFCASE

1. Choose a lightweight, weatherproof bag that zips closed so that the items in your briefcase will be protected in all types of weather.

2. Take what you need but not more than you need. If you travel by car, put some of the items you might normally put in your briefcase (office tools, minicassette machine, medical kit) in a separate bag that can remain in your car.

3. Don't dump things into your briefcase during the day. Have with you file folders ("Action," "To File," etc.) and envelopes for receipts so that you can sort the papers as you put them in. This will save you time when you return to your office.

THE CAR: YOUR MOBILE HOME OFFICE

1. Set up a mobile office for your car, complete with file folders, desk supplies, and stationery and envelopes. Store these things in a portable file box you can leave in the back of your car.

2. To make calls from the road, make safety a priority. Pull over to

call, let a passenger dial for you, or invest in a phone system with voice-activated dialing and a speakerphone.

3. Keep your car in good repair. There's nothing that will inconvenience you more than a breakdown on the way to or from a business meeting.

BUSINESS TRAVEL

1. Planning ahead for business travel will help take the stress out of it. Have a basic packing list for yourself, and a "While I'm Away" checklist for those at home. Amend them as necessary depending on the circumstances of each trip.

2. When it comes to paperwork, pack the files you'll need for the trip itself and also take along any files you might need for "client emergencies."

3. Stay in touch by e-mail and voice mail, and keep up with your paperwork, organizing it neatly within your briefcase throughout the trip. That way you'll be able to hit the ground running when you get home.

THE FUTURE

1. To increase business, start gathering customer e-mail addresses, and begin giving out your own e-mail address as well by putting it on your letterhead and brochures and handing it out freely.

2. Start learning by going on the Internet whenever you have time. You'll learn of new services and products, and you'll get ideas about what makes a good Web site.

3. If you don't have a Web site, experiment by teaming up with someone who does.

ABOUT THE AUTHORS

RONNI EISENBERG, author of *Organize Yourself!* and the entire Hyperion "organizing" series, has given a multitude of workshops, lectures, and demonstrations across the country on how to get organized. She lives and works in Westport, Connecticut, with her husband and three children.

KATE KELLY, who co-authors Ronni's books and others, is a professional writer who owns and operates her own publishing business. She lives in Westchester County, New York, with her husband and three children.